EAST ASIA
Between Regionalism and Globalism

IMEMO is the Russian abbreviation for the **Institute of World Economy and International Relations**. It was established in Moscow in 1956 to study contemporary problems of global political and economic relations. It is a major think-tank within the Russian Academy of Sciences working initially for the Soviet and now for the Russian Government.

The **Institute of Southeast Asian Studies (ISEAS)** was established as an autonomous organization in 1968. It is a regional centre dedicated to the study of socio-political, security and economic trends and developments in Southeast Asia and its wider geostrategic and economic environment.

The Institute's research programmes are the Regional Economic Studies (RES, including ASEAN and APEC), Regional Strategic and Political Studies (RSPS), and Regional Social and Cultural Studies (RSCS).

ISEAS Publications, an established academic press, has issued more than 1,000 books and journals. It is the largest scholarly publisher of research about Southeast Asia from within the region. ISEAS Publications works with many other academic and trade publishers and distributors to disseminate important research and analyses from and about Southeast Asia to the rest of the world.

EAST ASIA
Between Regionalism and Globalism

Edited by **Gennady Chufrin**

ISEAS

Institute of Southeast Asian Studies
Singapore

IMEMO
Institute of World Economy and International Relations
Russia

First published in Singapore in 2006 by ISEAS Publications
Institute of Southeast Asian Studies
30 Heng Mui Keng Terrace
Pasir Panjang
Singapore 119614

E-mail: publish@iseas.edu.sg
Website: <http://bookshop.iseas.edu.sg>

ISEAS Library Cataloguing-in-Publication Data

East Asia : between regionalism and globalization / edited by Gennady Chufrin.
   1.   Regionalism—East Asia.
   2.   East Asia—Foreign economic relations.
   I.   Chufrin, Gennadi_Illarionovich.
HF1600.5 A1E13   2006

ISBN-13: 978-981-230-397-4 (hard cover – 13 digit)
ISBN-10: 981-230-397-9 (hard cover – 10 digit)

Typeset by Superskill Graphics Pte Ltd
Printed in Singapore by

Contents

Foreword

This book is the result of an agreement between IMEMO and ISEAS to translate into English from Russian a book written by IMEMO scholars about the Russian perspectives on the Asia-Pacific region. ISEAS agreed to publish it in the belief that it would help to inform and clarify what is the Russian scholarly community thinking and writing about the region.

Our region is in a state of flux, with the rise of China and the liberalization of India, as well as the revitalization of Japan. The United States continues to play a pivotal role in regional affairs. But what does Russia think about all these great changes, about the Russian role, and the impact of the changes like the holding of the East Asian Summit?

Russia at the moment seems to be withdrawn and preoccupied with domestic issues. Yet it has great potential to change the regional balance of power by adding its weight to that of another rising power, in particular, through its arms sales and energy supplies. Thus the region cannot and should not discount Russia, whose own rise is inevitable.

For very good reasons therefore, ISEAS had launched its ASEAN-Russia Dialogue, so as to open doors and create pathways of understanding between both sides. IMEMO has kindly agreed to be the partner of ISEAS in this endeavour of mutual discovery. Through a process of annual seminars, intellectual exchanges and book publications/translations, both Institutes hope to build a solid foundation for better relations and understanding. This translated book is a contribution towards the achievement of that goal.

I wish to thank our colleagues Mark Hong, Teo Kah Beng, and ISEAS intern Miss Kostetskaia Stanislava for their editorial assistance with this book.

K. Kesavapany
Director
Institute of Southeast Asian Studies
September 2005

Preface

This book is an abridged English-language edition of a monograph originally published in 2004 in Moscow, Russia. The monograph came about as a result of in-depth research into East Asian regionalism by a group of Russian scholars from the Institute of World Economy and International Relations (IMEMO) of the Russian Academy of Sciences. The English edition, although partly revised and updated, basically retained the logic and main ideas of the original text.

Professor Gennady Chufrin
Deputy Director
IMEMO

The Contributors

Vyacheslav B. Amirov is Senior Research Fellow, Center for Japanese and Pacific Studies, Institute of World Economy and International Relations (IMEMO), Russian Academy of Sciences. He has written numerous articles about Russia's role and interests in the Asia-Pacific region. His professional interests include Russia's relations with Asia-Pacific countries, economic integration in East Asia, Japan's and U.S. roles in the region.

Gennady Chufrin is Deputy Director, IMEMO. He joined the Russian Academy of Sciences in1978 and worked there at the Institute of Oriental Studies until 1998. In 1998–2002 he worked in SIPRI (Stockholm International Peace Research Institute), Sweden. He is an author/co-author of fifteen monographs and over 120 articles published both in Russia and abroad, in Russian, English, French, Japanese, and Korean.

Alexander Fedorovsky is Head of Section, Center for Japanese and Pacific Studies, IMEMO. He specializes in Korean studies and is the author of numerous articles and chapters in collective monographs on this subject.

Vilya Gelbras is Professor at the Moscow State University and concurrently Senior Research Fellow at the Center for Japanese and Pacific Studies, IMEMO. His professional interests cover socio-economic and political developments in modern China. He has published several books and over 200 articles on these issues.

Valentina Kuznetsova is an expert on financial aspects of economic development of Russia and China and has published over twenty articles and essays on these issues.

Alexander Rogozhin is Head of Section, Center for Development and Modernization Studies, IMEMO. He specializes in ASEAN studies and has published several dozen articles on the subject.

Victor Sumsky is Head of Section, Center for Development and Modernization Studies, IMEMO. He has worked in the Soviet Foreign Ministry (1975–79), Institute of Oriental Studies (1979–88), IMEMO (1988 to present). His areas of professional interests include political development of ASEAN countries, and international security in the Asia-Pacific region. He is an author of three monographs and contributed chapters to twelve books.

1
Regionalism in East Asia: Development in Stages

Gennady Chufrin

INTRODUCTION

East Asia, which includes China, Japan, North Korea, South Korea, Mongolia, and Taiwan in its northern part and Indonesia, Malaysia, Thailand, Singapore, Vietnam, the Philippines, Brunei, Laos, Cambodia, and Myanmar in the southern one, is universally accepted now as one of the most important regions in the world, both politically and economically. It is also characterized by an intensive growth of intra-regional economic ties and by the development of various political, security, and economic institutions on sub-regional and regional levels which make East Asia an increasingly more cohesive region. This is particularly impressive since only fifty years ago this part of Asia presented a loose assortment of colonial and semi-colonial states and territories which, along with China and the defeated Japan, were lying in ruins after the end of World War II (WW2).

REGIONAL DEVELOPMENT

1940s to 1950s

The initial stage of East Asia becoming a region with its own distinct characteristics covers the period from the middle of the 1940s to the end of the 1950s. The principal geopolitical and geo-economic changes that happened at that time in the Pacific basin were: (1) the transformation of the United States into a dominant political, military, and economic power in this part of the world after the end of WW2; (2) the collapse of the colonial system and emergence, as a result, of new sovereign states in Northeast and Southeast Asia; (3) acceleration of an economic decline — a process which started already on the eve of WW2 — of old colonial powers (the United Kingdom, France, the Netherlands, and Portugal) in East Asia; and (4) the simultaneous process of reorientation of economic ties of new East Asian sovereign states from their former colonial masters in Europe to the United States and its regional partners, foremost of all to Japan.

As a result of these fundamental changes a new, unprecedented type of political and economic relations started to emerge in East Asia which will help to create a basis for an eventual regional community. Already in the second half of the 1940s East Asian countries made their first attempts to begin an intra-state cooperation on economic issues. In this they were stimulated by similar goals of their socio-economic development, by the need to solve identical economic problems as well as by the existence of certain objective preconditions for the development of intra-regional economic ties (such as most of them being maritime states and therefore more easily accessible to economic contacts with their neighbours; the existence of traditional trade relations between different parts of the region; and the presence of the overseas Chinese business community in a number of regional countries.

Socialism *Versus* Capitalism

During the next several decades the process of regional economic cooperation in East Asia, while continuing to progress, underwent fundamental transformation under the impact of many political, social, economic, and ideological factors of national, regional, and even global significance. The most important among them was, undoubtedly, a prolonged confrontation between East Asian countries representing two antagonistic socio-economic and political systems — socialism and capitalism. Their confrontation often escalated to sharp conflicts, including armed ones, and made a highly destructive impact on all political and economic developments in the region. As a result of this confrontation East Asia became divided into two hostile camps confronting each other and remained split for many years. Under these conditions economic cooperation between regional countries divided on ideological and political grounds became extremely difficult and often completely impossible.

Apart from ideological and political factors East Asian countries became divided also by fundamental differences in their economic strategies. Those countries that were politically oriented towards the capitalist West developed on the principles of market economy, while those which declared socialism as their ultimate goal (China, North Korea, North Vietnam, and Mongolia among them) followed the Soviet-type model of centrally planned economy. These differences in economic models created, along with political and ideological contradictions, serious difficulties for regional countries in developing mutually advantageous economic cooperation. Sharp contradictions between them escalated even further as a result of the Korean War (1950–53), in which many regional as well as extra-regional countries, including the United States, China, and the Soviet Union, were involved.

1960s to Mid-1980s

The next stage in the formation of East Asia as a specific region covers the period from the beginning of the 1960s up to the middle of the 1980s. During these years the nature of regional development processes continued to be extremely complex. Indeed, the confrontation between the two opposing political and ideological camps continued to escalate. It culminated in two large-scale wars, one in Vietnam during 1961–75 and the other in Cambodia (three years later). Serious tensions, bordering on the resumption of hostilities, remained on the Korean Peninsula as well as in relations between China and Taiwan.

Also during that period relations between the Soviet Union and China became increasingly strained and finally underwent fundamental transformation. Their former relationship as political and ideological allies turned into a bitter confrontation and even into armed clashes on their common border.

These political, ideological, and military conflicts deepened the economic split among East Asian countries as well. Thus trade and economic relations between North Korea on the one side and the United States and its regional allies on the other were practically blocked. A similar situation existed in relations between South Korea and the Soviet Union with its regional allies. After Vietnam sent its troops to Cambodia at the end of 1978 its economic relations with most of its regional neighbours, including China, were broken. Vietnam's regional allies — Laos and Cambodia — found themselves in a similar situation.

And yet, with all these negative events, the majority of the East Asian countries started to get involved more actively in the development of regional political and economic ties. The process of their political consolidation was reflected in a number of security agreements signed on a bilateral or a multilateral basis. Also several sub-regional organizations were formed at that time in order to facilitate multidimensional cooperation among their members. These processes were developing most actively in Southeast Asia where, after several unsuccessful attempts, the Association of Southeast Asian Nations (ASEAN) was formed in 1967 by Indonesia, Malaysia, Singapore, Thailand, and the Philippines. As a result of growing intra-state cooperation and the strengthening of regional commercial, financial, investment, and other economic ties, the volume of regional trade in East Asia started to grow at an advanced rate and its share in the total trade turnover of regional states reached 35.1 per cent by the end of the 1980s.[1] It is worth noting in this regard that the growth of regional trade continued in the absence of any regional agreements on tariff or non-tariff reductions in East Asia similar to those that existed in the European Union. Large financial and banking centres of regional and even global importance were established in Tokyo, Hong Kong, and Singapore. From the middle of the 1960s the Asian Development Bank (ADB) began its operations in the region. At the end of the 1960s the Asian Dollar Market was formed in Singapore in order to meet the requirements of short-term and medium-term credits in regional countries. Within a very short period the amount of transactions registered on that market grew manifold.

Thus, the development and strengthening of regional economic cooperation continued in spite of the escalation of confrontation between two hostile political systems in the region and also in spite of serious internal political and economic contradictions within each of these systems. This only proved the existence of objective interests among East Asian countries in facilitating regional economic cooperation.

End of Cold War

In the middle of the 1980s the formation of the East Asian region moved into its third stage. Its beginning was marked by the first signs of normalization in global and regional political relations. They were followed by the end of the rigid confrontation between the two global ideological camps, and then by the end of the Cold War. As a result the basic direction in the development of international relations was no longer determined basically by ideological and military factors but increasingly more by economic ones.

These fundamental changes in international relations made a lasting impact not only on global political and economic developments which began after the end of the Cold War but also on the nature and substance of the processes of regional cooperation and integration started earlier in East Asia. The latter then progressed under much more favourable conditions, helping regional countries to come closer together on a constructive economic platform and not on a confrontationist political–ideological one.

The improvement in the political and security situation in Southeast Asia, which began at the end of the 1980s, resulted in the resolution of the Cambodian conflict and the end of confrontation between the six members of ASEAN and the Indochina states. These events were followed by all ten Southeast Asian countries finally becoming members of ASEAN. In Northeast Asia, China and South Korea began normalizing their bilateral relations, which contributed significantly to regional economic cooperation in that sub- region of East Asia as well. Sub-regional economic cooperation among the ASEAN countries was also progressing from being rather slow and mostly formal during the 1970s to becoming more active and more concrete during the 1980s and the 1990s. East Asian countries also demonstrated their growing interest in wider economic cooperation with other countries in the Pacific basin when they joined the Asia-Pacific Economic Co-operation (APEC) forum. At the 1994 summit meeting in Bogor (Indonesia), APEC member states, including those from East Asia, declared their intention to undertake measures for trade and investment liberalization as well as for enhancing economic and trade cooperation in the Asia-Pacific region with a view to establishing a free trade zone there. Two years earlier, that is, in January 1992, at the Fourth ASEAN Summit in Singapore it was decided, in addition to the already existing preferential trading arrangement (PTA), to establish the ASEAN Free Trade Area (AFTA) in Southeast Asia and after that, of customs union.

During this period regional economic and trade ties in East Asia continued to grow at a fast rate. As a result, by 1997 the share of regional trade of East Asian countries in their total trade reached 45.5 per cent.[2] A similar situation developed on the sub-regional level. Thus in 1985–97, the volume of mutual trade among the nine Southeast Asian countries (which, except for Cambodia, were already full-fledged ASEAN members by that time) increased more than six-fold and its value reached US$162 billion. Simultaneously its share in the total trade of Southeast Asian countries increased from 18.3 to 22.3 per cent. During the same years the volume of mutual trade between countries of Northeast and Southeast Asia increased by 4.7 times, reaching US$210 billion, while its share in the total trade of Northeast Asian countries grew from 9 to 13 per cent.[3] As a result the degree of economic interdependence of East Asian countries increased substantially. Worth noting was that it happened under conditions of stable and exceedingly high rates of economic growth.

Financial Crisis

However, in 1997–98 a serious crisis broke out in the region. It started from a financial and banking crisis in Thailand and South Korea and then spread to most other East Asian countries. As a result there was considerable reduction in their growth rates and a sharp fall in production. The economic crisis was followed by a no less severe political one, causing serious social upheavals and change of ruling regimes in a number of regional countries, including Thailand, South Korea, and the Philippines. The most painful consequences of this crisis were probably for the economy and political life in Indonesia, the largest country in Southeast Asia.

Causing fundamental changes in the political and economic climate in East Asia, the 1997–98 crisis marked the beginning of the next stage in regional development. One of the immediate consequences of the crisis was the revision of development plans in most regional countries. Contrary to their initially declared priorities of trade liberalization, the East Asian countries were forced, at least temporarily, to shift emphasis in their economic policies to restoration of their economic growth by protection of domestic markets and by securing financial stability. And yet, only two or three years after the crisis, the countries of East Asia turned back to the need of developing regional economic cooperation. However, they were now determined to proceed with its development no longer on the principles of "open regionalism" advocated by the United States, Australia, and Canada and typical of the APEC activities in the 1990s, but rather in accordance with the proposal of the Prime Minister of Malaysia, Mahathir Mohamad, originally made by him as early as in December 1990. He proposed at that time to establish an East Asian Economic Grouping (EAEG), consisting of the ten ASEAN member states, Japan, China, South Korea, and possibly Taiwan. This proposal met with sharp criticism from the United States and was interpreted there as an attempt to establish an economic bloc in East Asia on a plainly anti-American basis. It seemed, therefore, as if EAEG had no future.

Globalization

However, less than a decade later, starting from 1999, leaders of the East Asian countries found it possible and expedient to start multilateral consultations in the "10+3" format on the need of "establishing more close partnership in East Asia" on economic issues. They were pressed to do so by a variety of developments in international relations, ranging from the already mentioned 1997–98 East Asian crisis to the slowing down of global economic growth rates. The dissatisfaction of regional countries with the activities of APEC, which, in their opinion, was too large and too diverse for dealing with concrete problems, became a factor in the opening of consultations. But perhaps even more the revival of East Asian countries' interest in regional economic cooperation became influenced by globalization.

Indeed, globalization is known as the latest form of the continuing internationalization of economic life in the world. It was caused by a dramatic progress in global technologies, in particular in the development of modern information and communication technologies. Also globalization made a fundamental, though a disproportionate, impact on the development of individual countries and their growth rates. East Asian countries did not — and in fact could not — stay away from globalization. However, they experienced not only positive but also painful adverse effects of globalization. Thus it caused a lingering crisis of the East Asian development model that accorded a strong role to the government in national economies. Indeed following this model helped many East Asian countries — from Japan to Malaysia and Indonesia — to achieve impressive economic results from the 1960s to the 1990s.

Responding to new economic realities, East Asian countries decided to facilitate their economic cooperation in order, as it was stated at the ASEAN summit in Kuala Lumpur in October 2002, to protect their national interests by collective efforts. In particular, trying to prevent the repetition of crises similar to the one in 1997–98. They called for: (1) strengthening of regional cooperation in banking and finance in order to reduce risks of short-term foreign capital fluctuations; (2) working out mutually acceptable norms and regulations of banking operations that could be used in emergency situations; (3) reduction of tariff and non-tariff barriers in regional trade and its liberalization; (4) creation of favourable conditions for investment flows between regional countries; and (5) promotion of regional cooperation in science and technology in order to bridge the existing gap in economic development with advanced industrial nations in Europe and North America.

In other words, promotion of regional economic cooperation was considered in East Asia as a timely response to the challenges caused by globalization, while working out rules and regulations for regional commercial, investment, and financial cooperation — as measures aimed at improving the efficiency of their economies. Of course development of regional economic cooperation in East Asia was in no way and at no time considered by its participants as a counterweight to globalization. It was merely directed against the most negative manifestations of the latter and in fact was realized as one of the forms of globalization at a regional level.

Tendencies that developed in East Asia at the turn of the century in favour of regional and sub-regional economic cooperation were determined, along with these general considerations, also by the need to overcome concrete negative consequences of the 1997–98 crisis. Therefore their earlier declared trade liberalization programmes were reconfirmed. Also a number of concrete steps aimed at promoting regional economic cooperation were made by East Asian countries in the area of banking and finance. As a result the whole traditional structure of intra-regional economic relations started to change.

Free Trade Agreements

In regional trade these fundamental changes were linked to the signing by regional countries of several free trade agreements (FTAs) on bilateral and sub-regional bases. The FTAs introduced mutual tariff preferences as well as other benefits, such as the abolition of non-tariff barriers or setting common standards. For the first time in their history, the three most economically powerful regional nations, Japan, China, and South Korea — which not very long ago flatly refused to participate in any bilateral or multilateral preferential trade agreements — started to use FTAs actively in their economic policy. Similarly, ASEAN member states decided to proceed with the implementation of the earlier concluded AFTA agreement too. For that purpose the six economically advanced nations (ASEAN-6) committed themselves to reduce their tariffs in intra-ASEAN trade to zero level by 2010 while the other four ASEAN countries (ASEAN-4) pledged to do that five years later.

Meanwhile, the number of bilateral FTAs started to grow in East Asia. First, bilateral FTAs in the region were concluded between Japan and Singapore and also between South Korea and Singapore. They were followed by similar agreements that were either concluded or in the offing between Japan and Brunei, Malaysia, Thailand, Taiwan, and South Korea as well as between South Korea, Singapore, and Thailand. The surge in popularity of bilateral FTAs was explained by the fact that by concluding them, the participants expected that they would make a strong contribution to their national economic development. It is important to note in this regard that the terms of such FTAs often envisaged cooperation between their members far beyond simple tariff reduction. They provided also for the liberalization of trade in services, protection of investments, harmonization of standards, protection of intellectual property rights, coordination of customs procedures as well as establishing mechanisms for dispute settlements. Some of such FTAs envisaged bilateral cooperation on e-commerce that was actively developing in the modern epoch of information and communication technologies as well as on science, education, and environmental issues.

The spread of bilateral FTAs did not mean, however, that the regional countries had given up their plans of developing multilateral trade cooperation. Thus, along with facilitating an intra-ASEAN preferential trade regime, the Association's members reached an agreement with China at the end of 2001 on establishing a common free trade area within the next ten years. To stimulate ASEAN's interest, China pledged to reduce its import tariffs on a number of ASEAN commodities ahead of introducing similar procedures with regard to imports from other countries. One year later ASEAN and China signed a framework agreement on ASEAN-China economic cooperation that further advanced their cooperation. Following China, plans to conclude similar FTAs with ASEAN were announced by Japan and South Korea.

In November 1999 at a summit meeting in Manila, ASEAN floated the idea of establishing the East Asian Free Trade Area (EAFTA) that would consist of the ten members of ASEAN, along with China, Japan, and South Korea. One year later at a meeting in Singapore members of ASEAN developed further its original idea, proposing to set up a special working group that would consider concrete recommendations on EAFTA. If this idea of ASEAN is indeed realized and EAFTA is established, it would become one of the largest regional trade organizations in the world, along with the European Union and the North American Free Trade Agreement (NAFTA).

However, it seems that this goal will not be easy to achieve. The main obstacles for the formation of EAFTA appear to be: (1) serious differences in economic development levels between regional countries; (2) the existence of a large number of states among them with weak and highly unstable economies; and (3) the absence of mutually agreed regional mechanisms for the coordination of national financial and economic policies. Because of these problems, many less developed regional countries maintain strong scepticism regarding EAFTA and are wary about the possible consequences its creation may have for their economies. Even more important for EAFTA prospects is Japan's attitude to it that so far remains rather reserved. Indeed so far the political leaders and the business community of Japan show more interest in bilateral FTAs. At the same time it is China that has become one of the most active and consistent supporters of reaching a regional agreement on multilateral preferential trade in East Asia. In that case China obviously expects to strengthen its role in the regional economy.

Financial Cooperation

Along with the growth of trade cooperation, there has lately been a notable development of multilateral cooperation on financial issues. In 2000 Japan, China, South Korea as well as the ten ASEAN countries met in the small town of Chiang Mai in Thailand and agreed to create a network of the so-called "swap arrangements" in order to protect financial stability in the region as well as the stability of exchange rates of national currencies and to prevent any large-scale financial crises like the one which happened in 1997–98. Acting in the framework of this agreement (which became known as the Chiang Mai Initiative), the East Asian countries signed a number of bilateral cooperation agreements among themselves on financial and monetary issues. Thus Japan signed "swap" agreements with South Korea, Malaysia, Thailand, the Philippines, and China while China also signed, apart from Japan, similar agreements with Thailand, South Korea, and Malaysia.

Also, the East Asian countries plan to create additional mechanisms for ensuring financial stability in the region that may include an Asian Monetary Fund (AMF), originally proposed by Japan as early as in 1977 but rejected at that time under pressure from the United States.

CONCLUSION

The above-mentioned changes in regional economic cooperation in East Asia present sufficient grounds for making a conclusion that this process has significantly picked up its pace over the last decade. At the same time one has to admit that the results achieved so far are still lagging behind comparable achievements of the European Union. Nevertheless, realistically assessing the progress made in East Asia over the last few years, one may reasonably expect that already in the mid-term perspective changes in the structure of economic relations in this part of the world may have a lasting impact on the total system of global economic relations.

Further prospects, opportunities, and effectiveness of regional economic cooperation in East Asia will, however, depend on a wide variety of factors, both economic and non-economic. In particular, the future of this cooperation will depend heavily on the ability of the regional countries to reconcile their often highly conflicting political and security interests, or to put it differently, on the possibility of cooperation between tough political opponents. It remains unclear if common or similar economic interests alone may create sufficient basis for an effective multilateral economic cooperation while the positions of its potential participants on issues of national or regional military security are widely divergent. These considerations are very much relevant to the situation in East Asia, where regional economic cooperation was slowed down or even completely blocked for years on end during the Cold War period. Unfortunately even now East Asia faces serious political problems, such as an unresolved nuclear crisis on the Korean Peninsula or the continuing tensions in relations between China and Taiwan. It is logical enough, therefore, to believe that a notable improvement in the political climate in the region may help to facilitate economic cooperation in East Asia.

NOTES

1   Sources: *Statistical Yearbook for Asia and the Pacific, 1990* (Bangkok: ESCAP, 1991); *Statistical Yearbook for Asia and the Pacific, 1999* (Bangkok: ESCAP, 2000). Estimates do not include trade with Taiwan.
2   Ibid.
3   Ibid.

2

Economic Cooperation in East Asia: Main Directions, Dynamics, and Scale

Alexander Rogozhin

INTRODUCTION

The problems of economic cooperation in East Asia are quite numerous and many-faceted, but proceeding from the formulation stated in the introduction to this book we deem it advisable to consider only one, but obviously the most important, aspect thereof, namely the dynamics of this process in the region at the turn of the century in two principal spheres — foreign trade and investment.[1]

Indeed, even the preliminary analysis of factual data on the development of economic cooperation in East Asia enables one to suppose *a priori*, before carrying out a statistical analysis, that the main form of this cooperation in the region covers mutual trade and investment. Clearly, these are the two principal areas of economic cooperation that were the first to emerge and are the most developed. There is no doubt, however, that they are being complemented on an ever-increasing scale by mutual ties in other areas: services, technological exchange, labour migration, and others.

The majority of the researchers justly believe that throughout the past decade, at the turn of the century, the scope of mutual trade of East Asian countries grew significantly, and its pace accelerated in comparison with the period of the 1960s to the 1970s. It is also supposed that the investment activity in these countries is now focused to a greater extent than before on the East Asian region itself. As a rule, such assessments are based on isolated, random, unsystematic data, among which statistical proofs are preciously few. This chapter undertakes to create a more comprehensive picture of the development of intra-regional trade and investment ties in East Asia based on the analysis of extensive statistical data.

Mutual Trade

When analysing the mutual trade of East Asian countries, we studied the statistical data on foreign trade of the fifteen countries in the region for a sufficiently representative period — thirteen years from 1990 to 2002, which makes it possible to speak not about a short-term trend, but about the emergence of a long-term tendency in the evolution of the process under study. By this we mean the intra-regional trade turnover of East Asian countries.

To make the calculations more reliable, the average annual indicators of two five-year periods, 1990–94 and 1995–99, and one three-year period (2000–02) were used in the analysis of the intra-regional trade turnover of East Asian countries. Thus it became possible to largely avoid distortions arising from the comparison of annual indicators where the element of randomness is greater, as well as to level off their sharp fluctuations caused by the East Asian financial crisis of 1997–98. As a result of the analysis of statistical data on the development of foreign trade of countries in the East Asian region, we arrived at the following main conclusions:

1. Growth Rate of Intra-regional Trade

The growth rate of the intra-regional trade of East Asian countries in two out of the three periods under study (in 1990–94 and 2000–02) exceeded a similar indicator of their overall foreign trade, and in 1995–99 it was only slightly lower than the latter, which testifies to more intensive contacts of these countries in the sphere of trade (see Table 2.1).

However, during each of the three periods under study the situation was different. In 1990–94 a clear dominance of growth rates of the East Asian

Table 2.1
East Asia: Growth Rates of Foreign Trade, 1990–2002
(Average annual in percentages)

	1990–94	1995–99	2000–02
TURNOVER			
Total	9.3	4.0	−1.2
East Asian countries	12.9	3.9	1.2
EXPORT			
Total	9.4	4.8	−2.0
East Asian countries	12.9	3.8	−0.9
IMPORT			
Total	9.2	3.1	−0.4
East Asian countries	12.8	3.9	3.4

Sources: Calculated and compiled from International Monetary Fund, *Direction of Trade Statistics Quarterly,* Washington, D.C., March 2002, March 2003, June 2003 (for the period 1990–99 earlier issues of this publication were used); Asian Development Bank, *Key Indicators of Developing Asian and Pacific Countries,* 2003 (Manila, 2003). Taiwan data are cited from the materials of the Taiwan Bureau of Trade website (www.trade.gov.ru) with corrections according to national sources, whenever possible. When necessary, international statistics was used to check against national sources (mainly for Cambodia, Laos, Myanmar, and Vietnam).

region was observed: growth rates of mutual trade in the region in terms of turnover, export, and import significantly exceeded similar indicators of foreign trade as a whole. This period was the most favourable for the development of intra-regional trade, at least for its dynamics.

The period of 1995–99 witnessed a dramatic change of the situation with regard to growth rates of the foreign trade of East Asian countries: under the impact of a sharp deterioration of the general economic, in particular of financial, situation in the region growth rates of the intra-regional trade turnover went down 3.3 times, which exceeded a similar indicator of the overall foreign trade (2.3 times). It testifies, on the one hand, to greater vulnerability of the intra-regional turnover to external negative factors in comparison with other segments of the foreign trade turnover of East Asian countries. On the other hand, it is indicative of a weak link between political declarations of intent on expanding mutual trade, the number of which particularly increased in the second half of the 1990s, and the actual state of affairs in this sphere in the same period.

In the latest period (2000–02) the dynamics of the development of intra-regional trade gives reason to believe that against the background of the extremely unfavourable situation in the foreign trade of East Asian countries as a whole — it was decreasing by 1.2 per cent annually — their intra-regional trade, in contrast, was growing by 1.2 per cent. Though the intra-regional export of East Asian states was declining, the rate of decline was more than twice as slow as that of their total export (–0.9 and –2 per cent respectively). At the same time the import of East Asian countries from the region was increasing by 3.4 per cent per annum, while the overall import was dropping by 0.4 per cent per annum. Consequently the tendency for intra-regional trade growth to outpace that of total foreign trade in the above-mentioned period prevailed again.

2. Share of Intra-regional Trade

As seen in Table 2.2, the share of intra-regional trade in the total trade turnover of East Asian countries had a tendency to grow, confirming the fact of their increased interdependence in the sphere of trade. Throughout the whole period of 1990–2002 the share of intra-regional trade in the foreign trade turnover of East Asian countries was rising every year, from 46.5 per cent in the first half of the 1990s to 51.2 per cent in the first three years of the new century.

At the same time the average annual value of trade within the framework of intra-regional trade almost doubled in 2000–02 while the aggregate turnover of East Asian countries increased by less than 1–8 times. Furthermore, the annual intra-regional import of East Asian countries (see Statistical Supplement I, Table 1 and 2) regularly exceeded their intra-regional export (by US$32 billion, in 1990–94, by US$44 billion, in 1995–99; and by almost US$61 billion in 2000–02) — this fact may tentatively be accounted for by large-scale re-export operations of some countries and territories of the region (notably Singapore and Hong Kong).

Table 2.2
East Asia: Foreign Trade, 1990–2002
(Average annual)

	1990–94	1995–99	2000–02
Total foreign trade (US $billion)	1,716	2,598	3,059
Intra-regional trade (US $billion)	798	1,287	1,565
Share of intra-regional trade in total foreign trade (%)	46.5	49.5	51.2

Sources: Calculated and compiled from sources for Table 2.1.

3. Individual Countries

Individual countries of the region differ significantly by the extent of their involvement in intra-regional trade, showing differently directed dynamics of their participation in the process with separate tracks for export and import operations. Since the figures in Table 2.2 averaged for five-year periods may offer only a generalized picture of the role of intra-regional trade in foreign trade operations of East Asian countries, similar indicators for each of the fifteen countries under study have been calculated (see Table 2.3).

Firstly, in 1990–94 the share of intra-regional trade in the foreign trade turnover of six out of the fifteen East Asian countries exceeded the average level. In 1995–99 the number of such countries slightly decreased — to five, however, in 2000–02 it went up again — to nine, which confirms the trend towards involving most East Asian countries in regional trade integration.

Secondly, when considering the changing situation with regard to the participation of individual countries in intra-regional trade, it has become

Table 2.3
East Asia: Intra-regional Trade by Country, 1990–2002
(Average annual)

	Value (US $billion)			Share (%)		
	1990–94	1995–99	2000–02	1990–94	1995–99	2000–02
Brunei	3,237	3,828	3,683	68.9	71.7	77.7
Laos	354	674	842	69.7	67.0	73.3
Myanmar	1,272	2,627	3,674	71.6	71.0	70.0
Hong Kong	144,752	232,123	270,420	60.0	62.6	66.8
Indonesia	34,314	48,256	63,270	57.0	55.3	64.4
Vietnam	3,631	12,940	19,337	55.4	55.4	63.0
Singapore	81,873	138,416	149,714	55.8	57.8	59.7
Cambodia	615	1,516	1,770	65.4	75.5	58.1
Malaysia	48,062	83,937	99,855	57.0	55.9	57.6
Philippines	11,729	27,775	38,225	43.9	47.4	54.8
Taiwan	67,753	111,348	134,504	44.9	49.8	53.0
Thailand	38,319	59,381	67,932	50.5	50.6	52.0
People's Republic of China	99,689	171,030	254,544	58.3	54.2	47.6
South Korea	65,223	107,574	134,307	40.2	41.0	43.0
Japan	197,131	285,790	322,482	33.7	38.6	41.0
People's Republic of China including Hong Kong	244,441	403,153	524,964	59.7	58.7	55.9

Sources: Calculated and compiled from sources for Table 2.1.

apparent that eleven of them manifested a steady increase in the regional share in 1990–2002. And only two of them — Cambodia and the People's Republic of China (even with the inclusion of Hong Kong's foreign trade turnover data) — demonstrated a decrease in the regional share of their aggregate turnover.

A sharp increase in exports to the United States appears to have been the reason in both cases. It was particularly noticeable in Cambodia in 2000–02 when the U.S. share of its exports exceeded 60 per cent. It became possible thanks to a large inflow of foreign capital to Cambodia, mainly to its clothing industry, attracted by Cambodia's privileged status (the least developed among developing countries), which enabled the country to start massive exports from its territory, chiefly to the American market.[2]

China's export expansion to the U.S. market at the turn of the century is undeniable and well known. But with regard to China it may also be assumed that the country's position in East Asian markets somewhat weakened: the East Asian financial crisis as well as China's modest successes in overcoming the trade deficit with ASEAN countries during 2000–02 took their toll.[3] Hence the recent attempts by China to restore and strengthen its positions in countries of the East Asian region, particularly in the ASEAN zone, which in view of the above become more understandable.

Thirdly, it should be pointed out that in various East Asian countries and territories the situation with regard to the changing importance of the East Asian region in their export and import developed differently. Estimates show (see Statistical Supplement I, Table 1) that in 1990–2002 the share of East Asia as a commodity market grew for Singapore, the Philippines, and Thailand in Southeast Asia, and for Taiwan, Hong Kong, South Korea, and Japan in Northeast Asia. The share of countries of the East Asian region in exports from Brunei, Myanmar, Laos, Vietnam, Cambodia, and the People's Republic of China (even together with Hong Kong) decreased. The significance of this region as a commodity market remained unchanged for only two East Asian countries — Indonesia and Malaysia.

Similar estimates of imports (see Statistical Supplement I, Table 2) testify to the fact that the importance of the East Asian region as a source of necessary commodities rose for twelve out of the fifteen East Asian countries and territories. The share of this region increased substantially in the imports of Cambodia, Vietnam, Brunei, Indonesia, Taiwan, and Japan; moderately in the imports of Laos, the Philippines, and Hong Kong; and slightly in the imports of Myanmar, Singapore, and Malaysia. The share of countries and territories of the region remained practically unchanged in the imports of South Korea. And it is only in the imports of China (even jointly with Hong Kong) that the share of countries and territories of the East Asian region shrank.

As a result of the analysis of the prevailing trends in mutual trade among countries of the East Asian region we arrived at the conclusion that:

1. Growth rates of intra-regional trade at the end of the twentieth century, and the beginning of the twenty-first century were higher than those of foreign trade ties of the East Asian region as a whole.
2. During the period under study the share of the East Asian region in the total foreign trade of East Asian countries demonstrated a distinct tendency for growth.

Investment Ties

The statistical base for even an approximate description of the state of mutual investment ties in the East Asian region is clearly insufficient and imperfect. However, our method seems to be the only feasible one for achieving the desired result. It is an attempt to solve, on the basis of the available statistical data, the main problem closely linked with the principal goal of this research project, namely to what extent some East Asian countries attract investment from other countries of the region (and probably invest in this region) and what the trends of this process are.

It goes without saying that the investment situation in East Asian countries, unlike the situation in the sphere of mutual trade, differs significantly not only from country to country, but also from one sub-region to another. In Northeast Asia all the countries and territories act simultaneously and actively as both investors and investment recipients, whereas in Southeast Asia there are mostly investment recipients. Naturally, the scale of the investment activity of countries of the East Asian region is quite different as well, with Japan and Laos forming two opposite poles, with the rest of the participants in the intra-regional investment process in between.

It would not appear possible to present a generalized picture of the dynamics of this process not only because of great diversity and differences among the countries and territories of the region, but also due to lack of necessary information. It may be known on good authority that this or that phenomenon exists, but to describe it even in the most general terms does not seem feasible. For example, Brunei is known to be a world-class investor and its returns on foreign investment have for a long time surpassed export earnings from the main export of the country — oil and gas. However, data on Brunei's capital investment have never been published and it was only under the pressure of its ASEAN partners that the country had to disclose information on its direct investment in member countries of the association. But it did no more than that. It is also known that Singapore is a major investor not only in East Asian countries. However any information on Singapore's foreign investments is deliberately published with a delay and is half-closed. The situation with regard to foreign investments of the People's Republic of China and Hong Kong is even more obscure. The same is true about capital investments in China itself.

It is known that foreign investments in some industries of East Asian countries are made on quite a large scale, but the relevant information is either not published at all or published in a way that prevents any analysis, including that of investor countries. Thus Indonesia did not publish information about investments in its oil and gas sector for a long time. Finally it has been made public, but only in the form of the overall investments of foreign companies in the above-mentioned sector. It is known beyond doubt that among companies investing in the development of Indonesia's oil and gas fields there are quite a few Japanese, Malaysian, Singaporean, Taiwanese, and other companies from the East Asian region, but it is impossible to determine the extent of their participation in the investment process, even roughly. It may be assumed that corresponding operations are not entered on Indonesia's balance of payments and are not included in the open statistics.

Even in the most developed countries and territories of the region investment statistics are either far from perfect or closed. For example, Taiwan publishes sufficiently detailed information on the direct investment of Taiwanese companies abroad; however publications with regard to foreign investments in Taiwan offer data on only two groups of investors: "investment of overseas Chinese" and "other foreign investment".

Taking into account the above-mentioned facts, the only way to determine quantitatively with a greater or lesser degree of accuracy how stable and dynamic investment ties of an East Asian country are with other countries of the region is to establish a specific share of investment from those countries in the overall inflow of investment to an individual country. The available statistics have not always made it possible to determine this indicator for comparable periods, which drastically limits the chances of discovering a certain trend — more often than not one can speak only about a rough estimate. However, this estimate, considering the state of the investment statistics in the East Asian region, is rather interesting.

The situation with the inflow of foreign investment to Southeast Asian countries is more or less clear. The ASEAN Secretariat's information base gathered bit by bit since 1996 makes it possible to draw some conclusions about the development of investment ties of Southeast Asian countries with their ASEAN partners as well as with other countries and territories of the East Asian region. In 2002–03 the ASEAN Secretariat for the first time published statistical sets reflecting the inflow of foreign direct investments (FDI) of the main investor countries according to their balance of payments, that is, real investment. The uniform system of the data and their correlation are of particular value. Unfortunately they cover the period only after 1994 (for details see Table 2.4).

Figures for all ten Southeast Asian countries, taken together, have shown that in the period of 1995–2001 countries and territories of the East Asian region accounted for 37 per cent (over US$59.8 billion) of the total inflow of FDI. The value of FDI in the region dropped more than 2.8 times — from US$11.7 billion to US$4.1 billion during the period (Table 2.4). However, the dynamics of the process differed considerably from one period to another.

In the period before the East Asian financial crisis the indicator under consideration clearly tended to grow, reaching its peak in 1997 — over US$16 billion (more than 49 per cent of the total FDI inflow). Further on up to 2000 it plummeted in absolute and relative terms. The reversal of the process has started only in 2000. In 2001, though the direct investment value was almost equal to that of 1998 (with the lowest since the 1994 share of the region in FDI amounting to 16.8 per cent), the share of the East Asian region in the FDI inflow to Southeast Asian countries almost doubled, constituting

Table 2.4
Southeast Asia: Inflow of Foreign Direct Investments, 1995–2001
(According to balance of payments)

	Foreign Direct Investments			
	Total		From East Asia	
	US$ million	%	US$ million	%
1995	26,348	100.0	11,704	44.4
1996	29,450	100.0	11,886	40.4
1997	32,746	100.0	16,092	49.1
1998	22,748	100.0	8,756	38.5
1999	24,221	100.0	4,062	16.8
2000	11,627	100.0	3,135	27.0
2001	12,823	100.0	4,130	32.2
Total	160,564	100.0	59,815	37.3

Source: Calculated and compiled from ASEAN Secretariat, *Statistics of Foreign Direct Investment in ASEAN* (2002).

32.2 per cent. The trend is obvious — as the economic situation in Southeast Asia improves, the influx of capital investment from countries/territories of the East Asian region to the former increases.

Another trend may be ascertained: as far as the FDI inflow to Southeast Asia in general and from East Asia in particular are concerned, four countries — Singapore, Malaysia, Thailand, and Vietnam — are far ahead. In 1995–2001 they accounted for 85 per cent and 83.4 per cent respectively of total FDI. The Philippines and Indonesia followed, but the gap was considerable.

When analysing the situation in individual countries of the sub-region, a third trend should be pointed out. According to the level of the participation of investors from countries/territories of the East Asian region in the FDI influx to Southeast Asia, the latter consists of three unequal groups. The first group is made up of Laos and Vietnam where such investors predominate. Laos accounts for almost 90 per cent of the FDI inflow from regional investors, Vietnam — for over 65 per cent. The second biggest, and probably most typical, group of countries includes Thailand, the Philippines, Malaysia, Myanmar, Indonesia, and Brunei, where the share of regional investors in the inflow of FDI varies from 32 per cent to 43 per cent. Singapore is the only country that belongs to the third group with the share of 22.5 per cent in which Japan alone accounts for 13.7 per cent of the total FDI inflow.

To assess the scale and tendencies of the development of East Asian investment ties with Japan we managed to bring in three indicators. Two of them do not reflect the dynamics of the process, but give an idea about its scale.

1. Countries/territories of the East Asian region account for 18.4 per cent (US$561 billion) of the total amount of Japan's accumulated FDI which constituted (US$3,056 billion) at the beginning of 2003. In Northeast Asia Japan's biggest direct investments are in China (US$24 billion), Hong Kong (US$55 billion), and South Korea (US$53 billion). In Southeast Asia the obvious leaders are Singapore (US$104 billion), Thailand (US$63 billion), and Indonesia (US$56 billion).
2. In the total amount of FDI in Japan the share of East Asian investors constitutes only 4.7 per cent (US$36.8 billion). Hong Kong, Taiwan, and Singapore are the leaders with 4.3 per cent (US$33.2 billion).

Undoubtedly, the amount of Japan's foreign investment is quite substantial for recipients in the East Asian region. However, it should be admitted that for Japan itself its investment efforts in countries of the region, as well as the investment of those countries in Japan, mean a lot less.

It is borne out by the third indicator — the most recently published comprehensive data on the inflow of Japan's direct investment to countries of East Asia in 1995–2000. Out of Japan's direct investment 17.1 per cent was placed in these countries during the above-mentioned period, with the share of the East Asian region changing in full conformity with the development of the East Asian financial crisis: it began shrinking as early as in 1997 and reached the lowest level in 1999 (10.4 per cent).

Quite a different picture emerges in the analysis of the role played by direct investment from countries/territories of the East Asian region in China. Even the limited information which we have at our disposal for 2000–02, testifies to a steadily high share of these countries/territories in the FDI inflow to the People's Republic of China: on average it constituted almost 77 per cent and remained unchanged throughout the whole period.

An interesting peculiarity of China's investment policy is the active use of direct foreign investment from offshore zones — their exotic origin, however, barely conceals the actual source of the capital from the British Virgin Islands and the Caymans. This is primarily either the capital of Taiwanese high-technology companies which in this way circumvent the laws limiting their investment activity in mainland China or the Chinese capital proper that was exported from the country in full or partial compliance with the rather strict national legislation and then acquired a new, more protected status at home positioning itself as foreign capital (that is, having gone through the procedure called "round tripping"). In any case these are capital investments the initial source of which was mainly the East Asian region.

It is every bit as true with regard to the inflow of foreign investment to Hong Kong. Judging by statistical data for 1999–2001, on average, Hong Kong accounted for almost 89 per cent of the FDI inflow from countries/territories of the East Asian region during that period, with almost 78 per cent from Northeast Asia. Offshore zones play an even bigger role in FDI in Hong Kong. They averaged about 53 per cent of the total inflow (the leaders were the British Virgin Islands and the Bahamas). There is no doubt here either that the initial source of these investments is mainly the East Asian region.

The analysis of Taiwan's rather detailed investment statistics for 1995–2002 has made it possible to draw a conclusion about the priority role of the East Asian region as a zone for the application of Taiwanese capital. Out of US$48.2 billion invested by Taiwanese companies abroad during this period almost 57 per cent was invested in countries/territories of the East

Asian region. Naturally, a major part of these resources (over 46 per cent) was invested in the People's Republic of China and 7.4 per cent — in countries of Southeast Asia. Taking into account the fact that huge amounts of Taiwanese capital, having gone through offshore zones under various covers, came back to the region (and first and foremost to China) it becomes clear that Taiwan's investment ties with the East Asian region are getting increasingly stable.

East Asia's share in the overall volume of Taiwan's foreign investment underwent sweeping changes: having reached the maximum level of 71.2 per cent in 1997, in 2002 it shrank to the lowest point of 43.7 per cent. Then, however, there was a surge of investors' interest in investment opportunities in the East Asian region, and in 2002 East Asia accounted for over 70 per cent of Taiwan's FDI — this indicator came close to the 1997 maximum.

This tendency is quite naturally accompanied by the continuing decline in the role of investment of the so-called "overseas Chinese" (most of whom live in the East Asian region) in the FDI influx to Taiwan. During the period of 1995–2002 it averaged just 3.5 per cent, while the tendency for its fall is clearly discernible after 1998 — "overseas Chinese" with their focus on Taiwan are no less than Taiwanese themselves oriented towards the huge potential of mainland China.

Finally, assessing the state of South Korea's investment ties with countries of the East Asian region, one can draw a conclusion from the relevant statistics for 1998–2002 that it also has a tendency for steady expansion. In 1998–2002 the share of the East Asian region in the inflow of FDI to South Korea already exceeded 26 per cent (US$15.6 billion), with the group of leading investors (traditionally headed by Japan) complemented in the period by Malaysia (7.4 per cent — second place after Japan) and Singapore (3.7 per cent — third place).

In 1999–2002 the countries and territories of the East Asian region became attractive to investors from South Korea again. The region's share of their foreign investments averaged almost 36 per cent and in 2002 this indicator for the first time exceeded the 50 per cent mark. At the same time, in contrast to the preceding period, South Korean investors shifted their attention towards the People's Republic of China, where their investments rose almost fourteen times — from US$481 to US$1,901 million respectively. The interest in investing in Southeast Asia, though, somewhat decreased.

Thus, at the turn of the century, the investment activity of practically all the East Asian countries, with the exception of Japan, became increasingly focused on the East Asian region.

Statistical Supplement I, Table 1

Share of Countries of the East Asian Region in the East Asian Countries' Export in 1990–2002
(Average Annually)

	Export of East Asian Countries/Territories to East Asian Countries/Territories (US$ billion)			Share of East Asian Countries/Territories in the Total Export of East Asian Countries (%)		
	1990–94	1995–99	2000–02	1990–94	1995–99	2000–02
Brunei	2,111	1,983	2,581	88.4	83.3	78.5
Indonesia	20,707	28,948	36,845	62.5	56.6	60.7
Singapore	35,832	66,813	74,068	51.7	56.3	57.8
Malaysia	23,265	41,412	52,104	55.3	52.9	55.5
Taiwan	35,785	57,701	69,918	44.4	49.6	52.2
Philippines	3,730	10,922	18,423	14.6	42.6	51.3
Thailand	14,375	27,508	33,403	43.0	48.5	49.4
People's Republic of China	53,446	92,550	137,814	61.0	53.7	49.2
Hong Kong	52,701	87,037	94,348	44.9	48.9	47.8
Myanmar	363	519	1,112	53.5	42.5	47.0
Laos	107	204	195	61.5	55.7	46.5
Vietnam	1,871	4,155	6,356	63.8	50.4	45.7
South Korea	31,728	58,481	72,010	40.5	43.8	45.1
Japan	123,196	169,935	176,515	36.2	40.8	40.9
Cambodia	124	381	239	45.1	56.1	16.4
for reference People's Republic of China including Hong Kong	106,147	179,587	232,162	51.8	51.3	48.6

Sources: Calculated and compiled from International Monetary Fund, Direction of Trade Statistics Quarterly, March 2002, March 2003, June 2003, Washington, 2002–03 (for the period of 1990 to 1999 earlier issues of this publication were used); Asian Development Bank, Key Indicators of Developing Asian and Pacific countries 2003, Manila, 2003. Taiwan data are cited from the materials of the Taiwan Bureau of Trade website (www.trade.gov.ru) with corrections according to national sources, whenever possible. When necessary, international statistics were checked against national sources (mainly on Cambodia, Laos, Myanmar, and Vietnam).

Statistical Supplement I, Table 2

Share of Countries of the East Asian Region in the East Asian Countries' Import in 1990–2002
(Average Annually)

	Import of East Asian Countries/Territories to East Asian Countries/Territories (US$ billion)			Share of East Asian Countries/Territories in the Total Export of East Asian Countries (%)		
	1990–94	1995–99	2000–02	1990–94	1995–99	2000–02
Cambodia	491	1,135	1,531	73.7	85.5	96.0
Myanmar	909	2,108	2,562	82.8	85.1	88.9
Laos	247	470	647	74.0	73.4	88.8
Hong Kong	92,051	145,086	176,072	75.9	75.3	84.9
Vietnam	1,760	8,785	12,981	48.6	67.1	77.2
Brunei	1,126	1,845	1,102	48.8	62.3	75.9
Indonesia	13,607	19,308	26,425	50.3	53.2	70.6
Singapore	46,041	71,603	75,646	59.4	59.2	61.8
Malaysia	24,797	42,525	47,751	58.7	59.0	60.1
Philippines	7,999	16,853	19,802	48.8	51.0	58.5
Thailand	23,944	31,873	34,529	56.3	52.6	54.9
Taiwan	31,968	53,647	64,586	45.4	50.1	53.9
People's Republic of China	46,243	78,480	116,730	55.5	54.8	45.8
Japan	73,935	115,855	145,967	30.2	35.9	41.1
South Korea	33,495	49,093	62,297	39.9	38.2	40.8
for reference						
People's Republic of China including Hong Kong	138,294	223,566	292,802	67.6	66.5	63.4

Sources: See table 1 in the Supplement.

NOTES

1   We deem it advisable to make a few preliminary remarks determining the
     subject, method, and aspect of our study before starting the analysis of economic
     cooperation in the East Asian region. The subject covers fifteen countries and
     territories of the East Asian region: five in Northeast Asia — the People's
     Republic of China, Hong Kong, Taiwan, South Korea, and Japan — and ten in
     Southeast Asia — Brunei, Vietnam, Indonesia, Cambodia, Laos, Malaysia,
     Myanmar, Singapore, Thailand, and the Philippines. The method of our study
     is primarily statistical. Our analysis is based on the use of the data on the state
     of **foreign trade** of all countries and territories of the East Asian region, published
     in yearbooks of the International Monetary Fund (*Direction of Trade Yearbook*),
     the World Trade Organization (*International Trade Statistics*), the ADB (*Asian
     Development Outlook, Key Indicators of Developing Asian and Pacific Countries*),
     Asia-Pacific Economic Co-operation (*APEC Economic Outlook*) as well as the
     United Nations Conference on Trade and Development's information on
     investment flows in the region (*World Investment Review*). Whenever possible,
     they were checked against the information on the state of foreign trade and
     foreign investment published in the above-mentioned countries and territories.
     Basic tables are presented in the supplement to the monograph, analytical ones
     are placed in the text. Some discrepancies in the figures summing up the results
     in the tables are due to rounding. "O" in the tables confirms the fact of a trade
     or an investment operation the value of which is less than US$1 million.
            The chronological framework of the study with regard to the analysis of
     trade ties in the East Asian region is sufficiently broad — from 1990 to 2002,
     which makes it more credible. However, with respect to **investment contacts** of
     countries in the region the options for the period of study were much more
     modest, from 1995 to 2002. In doing so we had to be guided exclusively by the
     availability of relevant information that so far has not lent itself to unification
     either by individual specialists, or by the staff of the statistical services of
     countries in the East Asian region. Besides, for the analysis of investment ties of
     countries in the East Asian region we had to resort (in contrast to the analysis of
     trade) to different, often incomparable sources for sub-regions: more or less
     unified for Southeast Asia and unsystematic for Northeast Asia.
            It should also be noted that the statistical information on regional economic
     cooperation prepared in countries of the East Asian region differs not only by its
     volume, structure, and quality (first of all, degree of credibility), but also by the
     principles of data tracing and standards of their registration. For example, in
     Laos the record of foreign trade operations is extremely unsatisfactory. Cambodia
     is the only ASEAN member where foreign trade operations are not entered on
     the balance of payments. Singapore and Malaysia keep detailed accounts of the
     above-mentioned investments, but they publish only part of the information
     about them (mainly about the investments in the manufacturing industry).

Myanmar's foreign trade statistics do not reflect half of actual operations, and even the officially published data are constantly reviewed. Singapore's customs statistics make one overjoyed with its comprehensiveness, whereas data on the capital transactions in the country's balance of payments are presented in the most general way.

It is not accidental that all the leading integration associations in the region, in particular the Association of Southeast Asian Nations and APEC, recognize the necessity for speedy unification of statistical information. ASEAN has already made certain progress in solving this problem — its statistical units, supported by the national statistical services, have formed relatively full and comparable databases on mutual trade and investment of the ASEAN member countries, while in APEC the process is still dragging on.

Undoubtedly, in the process of the formation of large-scale databases on the mutual trade and investment in the East Asian region one faces a lot of objective obstacles, starting from the fact that the process of registering foreign trade and capital operations is carried out by different institutions in various countries, more often than not, by several bodies in one country and sometimes even registration periods and the currency of accounting do not coincide.

With regard to trade numerous problems arise due to an imperfect statistical base in many East Asian countries and the objective difficulty of estimating commodity flows when a considerable part of those are in-house deliveries with the use of transfer prices. The conditional character of statistical data on foreign trade of many East Asian countries, especially Indonesia and the People's Republic of China, is to a great extent connected with the spread of smuggling, the volume of which is sometimes equal to, or even exceeds that of official trade (Myanmar is a case in point).

The true scale of the East Asian foreign trade is also difficult to determine in view of a supposedly big share of operations with a number of specific commodities, first of all armaments and narcotics. The information about them is either totally lacking or is purely subjective. It is technically difficult to study commodity flows in the region due to the existence of two large centres of intermediary trade — Hong Kong and Singapore engage in re-export operations on a large scale. Particular difficulties sometimes arise in assessing the scale of actual trade and investment cooperation between individual countries/territories. Singapore, for example, traditionally does not publish data on trade with Indonesia. Malaysia and Singapore conceal information on mutual capital movement. The estimates of the volume of trade and investment exchange between the Chinese People's Republic and Hong Kong raise quite a few questions.

As for the investment statistical data, they are far more imperfect than those of foreign trade. As a rule, they are offered on the basis of approved investments, which often reflects just the intentions of investors — information on actually realized capital investments (with few exceptions) is not published. Data on actual investments are often not cited from the balance of payments figures, but are published by various regulatory bodies in accordance with their own methodology. Considerable discrepancies in the estimates of the amount of investments occur due to the fact that they are registered by various bodies with different tasks and their own methods of registration (these are central banks and ministries of finance, economics, industry, and trade as well as agencies regulating the activities of foreign investors, for example).

These discrepancies to a considerable extent hamper the efforts of East Asian countries aimed at enhancing the investment attractiveness of the region. Since 1999 the Southeast Asian countries, members of ASEAN, have undertaken to form a unified database on foreign direct investment in the economy of the association's member countries, including the mutual one. These data taken from the balances of payments give the most accurate picture to date, of the real inflow and outflow of direct capital investment in the ASEAN zone. It is these data that are used in this chapter to clarify the question of the investment attractiveness of the East Asian region.

It is particularly noteworthy that the published investment statistics of practically all countries of the East Asian region concern only direct investment — the statistics of the portfolio investment movement in the majority of these countries, if maintained, are not published (we managed to come across uncoordinated information on the portfolio investments of Japan, South Korea, and Singapore; however, figures are usually presented without a detailed breakdown by the country).

Taking into account the aforesaid, we consider it necessary to stipulate that our attempt to analyse the main directions of regional economic cooperation by the statistical method is of a tentative character and cannot present the full picture of that cooperation. Among the reasons is the fact that many statistical data, for example, on foreign trade (detailed customs statistics) or capital movement (extensive balance of payments) were unavailable or closed either in principle or out of financial considerations (they are realized only on a commercial basis). It turned out to be technically impossible to carry out such kind of analysis of some directions of economic cooperation in the East Asian region where its expansion can be assumed. These are, first of all, such phenomena as labour migration and cooperation in the service sphere (tourism, transport services, and technological exchange). The available information on the development of regional cooperation in the above-mentioned spheres is fragmentary, scanty, and practically incomparable.

2   At present in Cambodia's clothing industry there are 185 enterprises, mainly small and medium-sized, employing 220,000 people. Out of this number only twenty three are Cambodian-owned, among the others almost 90 per cent of the factories were founded by entrepreneurs from Hong Kong, China, Taiwan, and Singapore (*Development Outreach*, July 2003, p. 4). No less than three quarters

of the Cambodian clothing industry's products are sold in the U.S. market. In order to avoid competition with similar Chinese goods a narrow niche was chosen where Chinese are not so competitive — manufacture of men's shirts. However, even in this area competition is quite high (with similar goods made in Macao), but so far labour costs in Cambodia are lower than in Macao, which enables Cambodian goods to find a ready market in the United States in the segment of medium-quality products.

3   According to our estimates the aggregate trade balance of China with ASEAN countries in 2000–02 had a very high deficit: in 2000 — US$4,605 million; in 2001 — US$4,645 million; and only in 2002 did China manage to reduce it to US$1,664 million.

3

Foreign Economic Strategy of China

Vilya Gelbras and Valentina Kuznetsova

INTRODUCTION

The Chinese People's Republic has been consistently developing its foreign economic strategy over the last twenty-five years of reforms and "openness policy". A basic outline of the strategy and its contents became known publicly in the 1990s as the relationship between the government of China and the elite of Chinese business emigration deepened and intensified. In its present form it is related to the speech that the former President of China Jiang Zeming made at the Third All-China Congress of the People's Representatives in the spring of 2000. The strategy of China's global foreign economic offensive, which became known as the "go global" and "inviting to come" policy was finalized by that time. In the wake of the Congress several publications were issued in China dealing with specific aspects of this strategy. They included excerpts from the Jiang Zeming speech but without any direct reference to it.[1]

According to numerous Chinese publications issued before the sixteenth Congress of the Communist Party of China (CPC) in 2002 this strategy was directed at transforming China into the most economically powerful nation in the world by 2020–30.[2] Although this target was not formally declared at the Congress, calls to "go global" and "inviting to come" were actually used as political directives. The sixteenth party Congress set the target to increase China's gross domestic product (GDP) fourfold by 2020 since in the opinion of Chinese economists it was such rates of growth that were required to overtake the United States as an economic power.

Preparation of the advanced growth strategy of China was started in the 1990s. It is impossible to state now to what extent this activity was connected with the formation of the World Chinese Businessmen Forum (WCBF). However, it is quite evident that China's government policy and the activities of the WCBF exerted significant mutual influence.[3]

The amount of direct foreign investments made in China sharply increased immediately after the First WCBF Congress. As Figure 3.1 indicates, the emergence of the WCBF evidently facilitated foreign capital flow to China. A considerable part of these investments were provided by *Hoa kieu Overseas Chinese*.[4] It demonstrated to other potential foreign investors that investments in China were profitable and the risks involved were reasonable. The volume of investments and the number of projects varied from one year to another

Figure 3.1
China: Projects and Corresponding Foreign Investment, 1979–2002

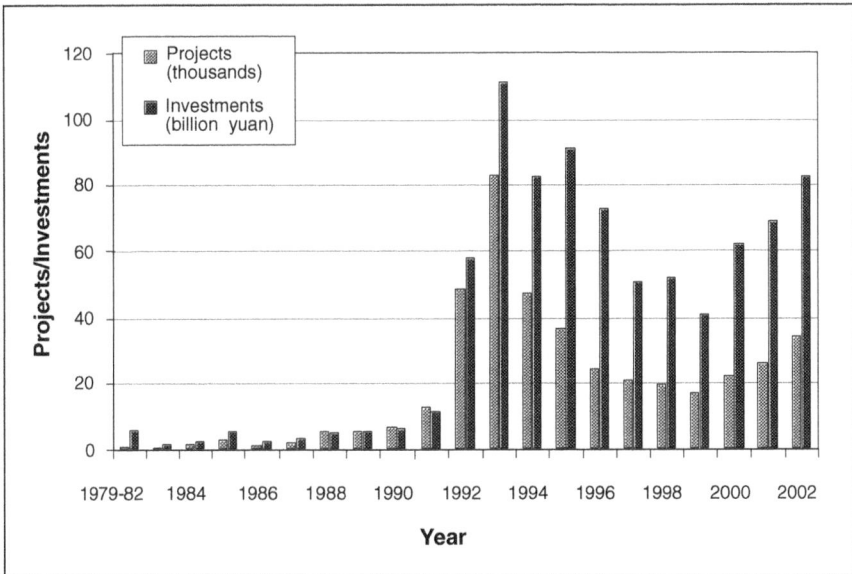

Source: Zhongguo tongji zhaiyao, 2003. — Beijing: Zhongguo tongji chubanshe, 2003. — E 167.

under the influence of various domestic and international factors but they never fell below the level of the 1980s to the early 1990s.

Simultaneously work was started in Beijing on researching concrete aspects of the national economic strategy aimed at a fast transformation of China into the largest economic power in the world. In 1997, at the Fifteenth CPC Congress, it was decided that promotion of an export-oriented strategy, along with further development of other aspects of international economic activities, were necessary for this purpose. In particular the Congress decided to create large-scale Chinese transnational corporations, to form a globally oriented complex trading system, to begin export of capital, as well as to use a policy encompassing "two markets" and "two raw material sources" (domestic and foreign).[5] Three years later these directives became an integral part of the strategy of global economic offensive, forming its basis.

By early 2000s this economic strategy was basically completed. Jiang Zeming spoke about it in 2000 during his visit to Guangdong, the main foreign trade base of China. He said:

> After twenty years of conducting reforms and "openness policy" we have achieved a remarkable success. As the Chinese economy progresses and its modernization advances, we have to facilitate implementation of the "go global" strategy …. Conditions for its implementation have become much better and the need for it is more pressing. China's future entry in the World Trade Organization will provide additional possibilities to implement this strategy. We must use this opportunity and "go global", advancing our enterprises into the international economy. Implementation of this strategy will help to further improve the national economic situation and promote our country's long-term development.[6]

Meanwhile studies of various aspects of international policy and economy continued in China. Special attention was paid to the role of China's main comparative advantage, that is, its abundant resources of cheap labour, and the "go global" strategy was formulated in such a way as to use this advantage to the maximum. "Implementation of this strategy will seriously help to advance the 'openness policy' to new levels, to create conditions for an optimum use of resources in domestic and foreign markets, and will play an important role in the gradual creation of our own large-scale enterprises and transnational companies," said Jiang Zeming.[7]

At the Sixteenth Party Congress goals, terms, and contents of "the third historic step" were modified without much discussion. It was decided to carry out "two double increases" (two successive twofold increases of China's GDP, which constituted the substance of "the third historic step") not within fifty (as had been originally proposed by Deng Xiaoping) but within twenty years. The goal of reaching an "average global prosperity level" was replaced by the goal of achieving the top place in the world economy while reaching an "average global prosperity level" was postponed until the year 2020. All these changes were explained by the need to serve a "great renaissance of the Chinese nation".

Stages of Realization of the "Go Global" Strategy

Jiang Zeming called the implementation of the global economic offensive strategy "a principal battle".[8] He said:

> Only by bravely and actively "going global" shall we be able, firstly, to compensate our shortages in natural resources and market limitations; secondly, to increase export of machinery, equipment and other capital goods, to import more modern equipment and to develop new industries; thirdly, to gradually form our own transnational corporations in order to improve our position in global competition; fourthly, to promote economic development of third world countries, to upgrade the power of forces fighting hegemonism and to defend international peace.[9]

According to Chinese publications China has already started to implement "transnational economic management". Its foreign economic offensive is to be accomplished in several principal areas: foreign trade, foreign investments, and the creation of transnational companies. According to Chinese press reports there are going to be four stages in the implementation of this strategy.[10]

The first stage — creation of production groups. At this stage the hundred best production groups selected should receive state support and would be allowed to raise foreign investments and carry out export activities.

The second stage — developing export-oriented production groups. First steps of internationalization should be made. These steps should include: active promotion of direct export-import transactions and creation of sales infrastructure abroad; gradual expansion of direct investment activities abroad that would involve various forms of joint ventures, acquisitions, and company control; and sales of commodities processed and assembled in third countries.

The third stage — promotion of transnational activities of export-oriented production groups. That would involve the creation of units and branches abroad that would be closely linked to parent companies.

The fourth stage — formation of transnational corporations. At this stage the production groups' international activities should become more mature. Among these groups a comprehensive division of labour would be formed. Their holding companies would operate all over the world — their activities in research and development, production, and sales would cover the most profitable regions in the world.

The time between the years 2000 and 2010 was termed "a key period" for the implementation of the first two stages.[11] During this decade China was expected to build up a group of export-oriented companies that would "gradually push back" the world's 500 largest multinationals in international business. During this decade the annual growth rate of China's foreign trade was forecasted to be 8.5–9 per cent. The export and import trade was planned to be mainly balanced. The foreign trade turnover was expected to reach US$20 trillion by the middle of the twenty-first century, that is, it would increase almost fifty-fold. It is clear that even a partial success of this plan will have a fundamental impact on the world economy.

Such were the plans at the time when the foreign economy strategy was originally formulated. In 2001–04 it was partially modified. While previously only state enterprises and joint companies with foreign capital participation were allowed to carry out foreign trade activities, now similar rights were granted to private companies, the so-called "people's enterprises" and individual producers. These changes would allow the high growth rates of foreign trade and foreign capital inflow to be maintained.

However the implementation of the foreign economy strategy was also accompanied by bureaucratic distortions. For example, it was reported that the authorities in some provinces, cities, regions, and even small districts had started selecting their own fifty, hundred, and even 500 companies, expecting them to be able to "push back" the world's top 500 multinationals.[12]

Practical Implementation of the Strategy

The officials who started a new "great campaign" in China are firmly convinced that their country is historically destined to be a world manufacturing plant and transnational enterprise. Their arguments are simple. No more than 12 per cent of the six-billion global population live in the industrially developed countries. China's population amounts to 1.3 billion people, that is, over 21 per cent of the global population.[13]

In declaring the "go global" strategy, Beijing uses its greatest advantage — a huge labour force — in global competition. Using its cheap labour for the production of low- and medium-quality industrial commodities, China sells them at the international market where these commodities have a strong competitive edge because of their low production costs, writes Jin Pei, deputy director of Industrial Economy Institute of the Chinese Academy of Social Sciences.[14] However, China's advantages in industrial export are largely limited to this group of commodities.

The shortage of domestic natural resources creates a serious problem. Shortages in oil, natural gas, and fresh water have become extremely acute recently. It was noted during a conference held in January 2001 that the problem of fresh water shortages might be resolved only by introducing new saving technologies while the shortage in oil and natural gas should be resolved by having ready access to the world's resources. At present China's dependence on the world's oil supply is very high, so China needs (like the United States) to create its own ninety-day strategic reserves and to have an access to other countries' oilfields.[15]

Among the issues related to the practical realization of the "go global" strategy the most topical ones under discussion now in China are the following:

1. Problem of managing state property abroad. It is clear that a comprehensive legislation regulating all important aspects of economic activities of state enterprises abroad (such as granting permissions for foreign investments, receiving credits, and establishing financial control) is required.
2. More specific definition of the "go global" policy. According to China's State Council development research centre this policy has to cover such areas as foreign investments for development of natural resources; industrial and agricultural production and processing; trade promotion; receiving of foreign contracts, research, and consulting orders; and the use of labour force, etc.[16]
3. Evaluation of the "go global" policy efficiency. That became particularly necessary after it was discovered that by the end of 2001 only one-third of companies allowed to operate abroad made profits, another third of them operated without losses but also without any profits, while the rest were unprofitable.[17] Such results came largely as a result of their management's over self-confidence and low professionalism.

At present the following models of "going global" enterprises exist in China:[18]

The first model — creation or purchase of companies abroad (such as Haier and TCL). Haier, for example, set up thirteen production plants in various economic regions of the world (in Eastern Europe, North and South America, the Middle East, and South Africa) and created industrial parks in the United States and Pakistan. The company established branches in Russia too. TCL invested over US$100 million in Vietnam starting production there of colour television sets and other electrical products. In 2002 TCL purchased facilities for producing up to 1 million colour television sets annually in Germany.

The second model — subcontracting (or outsourcing) for foreign companies. For example, businessmen from Chenzhou follow this model specializing in necktie production. The entire city does not produce any other goods now. Producing 250 million ties annually (about 30 per cent of its total world production) they sell them to foreign companies at US$2–5 a piece, while the foreign companies resell them for US$20–50 a piece. A similar system is used in the production and export of electro-technical tools. About 70 per cent of the world production is concentrated in China now, but the Chinese companies receive only 10 per cent of profits from their sales which are carried out by foreign companies.

The third model — producing goods for export domestically while using raw materials and components imported from abroad. Thus the Fuyao company makes automobile glass. About 90 per cent of the raw materials for this purpose are imported from Indonesia and Thailand while over 60 per cent of the finished products are exported. The share of the United States in its export sales is around 12 per cent, that of Australia 15 per cent, Japan 7 per cent, and Russia 10 per cent.

The fourth model — producing goods in China and selling them to foreign companies. For this purpose China set up "townships of small goods". Foreign companies have 160 purchasing offices in these townships. The volume of export from these townships doubles every other year. If the existing trend runs remain over the next few years, their total export may exceed 100 billion yuan. These townships may change into real international markets. Incidentally such townships are the main source of commodities sold to the Russian market.

The fifth model — buying shares in a foreign company. For example, a Chinese company Vansyan was among the first to test this model. It started by buying 21 per cent shares of an American company that was on the verge of bankruptcy for US$2.8 million. In return the American company undertook to purchase Vansyan products for the amount of US$2.5 million. As production costs in Vansyan were 30–40 per cent lower than in the American company, the transaction turned out to be mutually profitable.

The Size and Forms of Capital Export

Although the "go global" strategy has been declared only recently, the export of capital from China actually began long ago.[19]

The first stage (1979–83). During this period China started to realize its "openness policy" and develop foreign economic relations. Chinese investments amounting to US$45.73 million in sixty-one enterprises of twenty-three countries and territories were approved during this period.

The second stage (1984–88). This was a period when China began accumulate international economic experience, develop a national technical base, and of trained administrative personnel. The total number of enterprises set up abroad at that time with Chinese capital participation reached 450. The volume of Chinese investments reached US$665 million. The investments were made mostly in the production of iron ore, in the forest industry, fisheries, and industrial manufacturing.

The third stage (1989–93). During this period, 1,132 enterprises were established abroad. Total Chinese investments reached US$1,232 million. The largest share went into trading enterprises.

The fourth stage (1994–2000). By the end of 1999 China's State Council had approved almost US$7 billion of investments abroad. Out of these 60 per cent were invested in trading enterprises, about 20 per cent — in raw materials production, and 12 per cent — in industrial manufacturing. About 58 per cent of direct investments were made in Hong Kong and Aomen; 20 per cent — in industrially developed countries, and over 20 per cent — in developing countries and those with transitional economies, such as former Soviet republics and Eastern European countries.

The fifth stage. The current stage of the global economic offensive began in 2001.

In the opinion of officials from China's State Council development research centre the Chinese Government approves investments abroad for the amount of US$2 billion annually. However, these data reflect only part of actual Chinese investments made abroad because they do not include private investments and investments of financial organizations. The total volume of investments made abroad may therefore be substantially larger — to the tune of US$20 billion annually.[20]

An analysis of China's balance of payment data reveals huge differences in information on capital flows.

The capital outflow from China reached significant proportions in the 1990s to the early 2000s. Investigation's of cases including 4,000 officials, who had left the country by August 2004, revealed an outflow of US$50 billion.[21] Investigations of cases of over 500 people carried out by China's Ministry of Social Security (by May 2004) established an outflow of over 70 billion yuan.[22]

Information from China's former Ministry of External Trade and Economic Relations (METER) (since 2003 the Ministry of Commerce) sharply differs from the data of international organizations, in particular of the United Nations Conference on Trade and Development (UNCTAD).

The differences are very significant. They may be explained by the fact that METER's data were limited to officially approved investments, while UNCTAD took more sources into account. It should be noted also that the Chinese official data presented in Table 3.1 and 3.3 contradict each other. Their huge difference from the UNCTAD data means that conclusions

Table 3.1
China: Projects and Investments Abroad

By the end of year	Total Number of Projects	Total Amount of Investments	Chinese Investments	Growth in the Number of Projects	Growth in Chinese Investments
		US$ billion		%	
2000	6,296	11.2	7.6	—	—
2001	6,610	—	8.36	5.0	14.5
2002	6,960	13.78	9.34	5.3	11.7
2003 (1–4)	7,094	14.66	9.87	1.9	5.7

Notes: Approved by China's State Council and Central Government Ministries.
Sources: Compiled using the data from: http://drcnet.com.cn/html_document/guoyan/gybd/2002-09 19/127603drcnetchetechdfgdghdaA023.asp; http://drcnet.com.cn/drcnet/view_new.asp?dn=guoyan_drcindex1&cnt_id=0&mainunid=203819drcnetchentechdfgdghdaA023; http://hzs.mofcom.gov.cn/article/200306/200306/20030600097344_1/xml; http://drcnet.com.cn/html_document/guoyan/gybd/2002-09-19/127603drcnetchetechdfgdghdaA023.asp.

Table 3.2
Capital outflow from China, 1992–2001
(US$ *billion*)

	1992	1993	1994	1995	1996	1997	1998	1999	2000	2001
Errors and omissions	−8.27	−9.8	−9.77	−17.8	−15.56	−16.95	−16.58	−14.8	−11.9	−4.85
Total balance	16.34	7.25	17.44	24.98	9.64	36.47	38.64	30.39	—	—

Sources: 2002 Zhongguo touzi fazhan baogao — maisian guojihua de zhijie touzi kuangjia/Shanghai caijing dasue touzi yanjinsuo. — Shanghai: Shanghai caijing dasue chubanshe, 2002. — E 195; Zhongguo tongji nianjian, 2001. — Beijing: Zhongguo tongji chubanshe, 2001. — E 80; Zhongguo tongji nianjian, 2002. — E 82.

Table 3.3
China's Direct Investments Abroad, 1992–2000

Data Source	1992	1993	1994	1995	1996	1997	1998	1999	2000
METER (US$ million)	220	120	81	146	306	354	480	590	622
UNCTAD (US$ billion)	4.0	4.4	2.0	2.0	2.1	2.6	2.6	1.8	2.3

based on the official data cannot be considered as reliable. At the same time, these differences may indicate the existence of a great growth potential of Chinese investments abroad in the next few years because now both private businessmen and the so-called people's enterprises are allowed to carry out activities abroad.

The characteristics of China's capital export are:

1. Fast growth rate.
2. Investments over the last twenty years were made out in various areas — most of them in trading companies; but lately also in production of raw materials.
3. During these twenty years mostly small enterprises were established abroad; an average investment per company amounted to US$1.2 million only, which was significantly lower than an average investment per company made not only by businessmen from industrially developed countries (US$6 million), but also by those from developing countries (US$2.6 million).[23]

4. Investments were made in many countries all over the world but mostly in industrially developed countries of the Asia-Pacific region. Thus 45 per cent of their total amount was made in three countries — the United States, Canada, and Australia.

5. The main investment procedure was characterized by buying shares in foreign companies. At the same time, companies with 100 per cent Chinese capital were established. As a result, about 80 per cent of funds were spent on buying shares and the rest on establishing companies under complete Chinese financial control.

Financial Aspects of the "Go Global" Strategy

Both the implementation of the "go global" policy and the development of China's national economy require colossal financial resources. Among the most important aspects of financing the development goals a special role is accorded to the proper use of external economic relations. In this connection China undertakes considerable efforts to position its national currency as highly reliable at several levels: global, regional, bilateral, and domestic.

International Level

China is an International Monetary Fund (IMF) member and Chinese representatives sit on the Fund's board of directors. China presents itself in IMF as an exponent of developing countries interests. In the course of discussions regarding the IMF future status and its functions as well as regarding changes of the IMF Charter China demands to revise existing countries quotas, stands for the Fund transformation into a transnational institution functioning on a cooperative basis and opposes introduction of an automatic bankruptcy mechanism of sovereign debtors. This was stated by the former governor of People's Bank of China at the IMF autumn session in 2002,[24] and confirmed in autumn 2003 by its new governor Zhou Xiaochuan. He underscored that IMF had to look into methods of estimation of individual country quotas and revise them by taking into account fast economic growth of developing countries. In the opinion of China it would be impossible to increase developing countries representation in the IMF without such a revision.[25]

If China's proposals are supported by the majority of developing countries[26] and developed countries fail to unite against China the latter will get a chance to obtain a blocking number of votes in the IMF, thus undermining the position of the United States. These intentions of China proved to be quite real when confrontation aggravated between China and the United States on financial and economic relations in 2003. At the spring and autumn IMF sessions that year China's representatives openly accused the United States of conducting an economic policy that was increasing international economic risks. They demanded that developed countries, the United States in particular, should undertake responsibility for the reconstruction of the world economy; carry out structural reforms; increase deposit interest rates; stimulate domestic demand; regulate their trade policies; broaden the access of developing countries to their markets; and gradually resolve problems of their budget imbalance.[27]

In response the United States accused China of violating article 4 of the IMF Charter and of conducting a mercantilist foreign trade policy. Manipulating the yuan exchange rate by keeping it at a fixed level for an excessively long time and by limiting yuan convertibility China, in the American opinion, transfers the cost of its rapid economic growth on developed countries, especially on the United States. Americans maintain that the growth of Chinese trade balance surplus in trading with the United States leads to the growth of unemployment and of federal budget deficit in the country. Such policy makes a depressing impact on the American dollar and negatively influences the entire world economy.[28]

China's response to these accusations was rather sharp. The Chinese Government statement said that the United States and Japan should look for causes of their economic difficulties in their own countries. "Chinese economy can't permit itself not to develop. If Chinese locomotive is stalled, the same will happen to the rest of world". Demands for change of the yuan exchange rate would damage not only the Chinese economy but also economies of other countries, the statement said.[29]

Confrontation between the United States and China will hardly take a latent form again, because, among other reasons, of China's intention to continue undermining the U.S. influence in international financial institutions. In particular it is proved by China's stand on the issue of uniform behavioural methods and evaluation of activities of financial institutes.[30] China insists on participation of developing countries in formulating uniform standards, codes and legal procedures of business activities. China also insists on introducing new standards that would take into account differences between individual countries and allow these countries to introduce them themselves in accordance with local conditions.

Regional Level

China has been particularly active in this area during the last few years. Beijing invites attention of its regional partners to advantages they may receive trading with China. Promoting its investment attractiveness, China holds regular sessions of the Chinese Economic Forum in Boao (Hainan province). The forum was organized, on the one hand, as an analogue of the Davos World Forum and used to advance Beijing's own interests in the region. On the other hand the forum allows China to actively attract *Hoa kieu's* capital.

China proposed regional countries to form their own mechanism of resisting external economic shocks and of managing international capital flows. With that end in view it proposed several measures that later started to be realized. In particular China proposed regional countries:

• to co-operate in monitoring short-term capital flows;
• to introduce a system of bilateral currency swaps between central banks of ASEAN+3; and
• to control sovereign external debt.

China believes that unstable situation in principal world stock markets, corporate scandals in the United States and Europe as well as problems of the Japanese capital market will help the Chinese market to grow and to increase its influence on regional financial flows. Contrary to the opinion existing in Western countries that liberalization of the mechanism of setting interest rates is required to transform a national capital market into an international one, China is confident that it will be possible only with stable interest rates. That is exactly what happens in the Chinese market where all base interest rates are set by People's Bank of China.

In 2004 China's official currency reserves, including those of Hong Kong, exceeded US$609 billion, being second only to Japan's reserves. However, unlike the Japanese economy the Chinese one is on the rise. Beijing believes that none of the East Asian countries with the exception of China itself is capable of becoming a key financial guarantor of the region. Chinese financial authorities repeatedly underscore dangers of financial risks for countries with developing markets. According to Beijing, probability of losses for regional countries increases due to unpredictable fluctuations of developed countries' currency exchange rates. The use of a more stable currency for international settlements — meaning the yuan — may become a salvation for regional countries under these conditions.

Beijing believes that "the Japan era" in East Asian regional development has come to its end, while Japanese economy fundamental problems will seriously hamper the yen in participating in the competition for a future all-regional currency.[31]

Theoretically an exchange rate of a national currency aspiring to become a global or a regional currency must be sufficiently stable. It is exactly such policy that is conducted by the People's Bank of China over the last years. After a devaluation of the yuan of almost 60 per cent in 1994 its exchange rate is kept practically constant. The People's Bank of China allowed the yuan exchange rate to fluctuate only within a 1 per cent corridor.[32]

At present the share of China in East Asian regional export is less than 18 per cent (or about 30 per cent, including Hong Kong). But growth rates of trade between East Asian countries and China are very high. The financial sectors of many ASEAN countries are under *Hoa kieu* control. To link regional countries to its economy, China uses a wide variety of special measures aimed at stimulating its foreign economic activities. Most important among them are opening credit lines for import transactions as well as introducing settlements in the yuan in frontier trade or tourist business.

As a result, the yuan is already widely used in border trade between Guangxi-Zhuang Autonomous Region and Vietnam and Laos, Yunnan province and Myanmar, Inner Mongolia and Mongolia, as well as in trade with Russia, Kirghyzia, North Korea, and Nepal. Twelve Hong Kong banks started cash transactions in the yuan in 2004.[33]

Lately, China has consistently accumulated gold reserves, increased domestic gold production, and its import. According to official figures China's gold reserves in December 2001 reached 16.08 million of troy ounces. Now China is the fifth largest gold producer in the world and the third largest gold consumer. China's demand for gold tripled in 2004, when it reached 200 tons. In the next few years China's annual gold demand may reach 600 tons, according to experts from the World Gold Council.[34]

Regular trading in gold started in October 2002 at the Shanghai stock market. China expects it to become the most important site for trading in precious metals first at the regional level and then probably at the global one. Such a scenario carries out several advantages for China. Firstly, Shanghai will achieve the reputation of being principal regional financial centre and one of the leading financial centres in the world. Secondly, the capital inflow into China will increase and China will be able to step up its influence on financial flows in the region. Thirdly, the chances of the yuan becoming a regional currency will also significantly increase.

Plans to set up an AMF are now under active consideration in the region. This idea was originally proposed by Japan in 1997 but at that time it was turned down under the U.S. pressure. However, already in 2000 some practical steps aimed at its implementation were made. The plans under discussion propose to create a regional analogue of SDR (Special Drawing Rights). These proposals correlate favourably with plans for formation of an all-regional free trade area (East Asian Free Trade Area or EAFTA). Some steps in this direction have already been made. Thus, in spring 2003 the Central banks of eleven East Asian countries agreed to establish an Asia Bond Fund.

At the same time the creation of the AMF faces a number of serious difficulties. Firstly, it is necessary to bring into agreement interests of various countries. This may be achieved after long negotiations while regional countries already show their interest in having an alternative to both the U.S. dollar and euro. Secondly, success of such an agreement will depend on the willingness of countries — future AMF members — to conduct a co-ordinated monetary and fiscal policy.

Under these circumstances the yuan may have the chance to become a regional currency and China systematically pursues this goal. It also tried to make Shanghai one of the most important financial centres in East Asia. These plans may indeed become a reality. Such a conclusion is based on at least two considerations. China has succeeded in forming its international image as a reliable partner, of the country being politically and socially stable. The Chinese market possesses a great growth potential, attracting huge investments in the country. There is now no multinational corporation that has not already opened or plans to open its branches in China.

At the same time, domestic monetary and fiscal policies may not allow China to realize its global economic plans. A probability of China becoming a principal regional financial power will in many respects depend on the continued success of its domestic economic development and social stability. Over the last twenty-five years, China has indeed succeeded in significantly increasing its GDP and its economic power. However, the country faces a lot of serious problems. For example, the goal "to liquidate poverty" is still topical. The "go global" strategy is unable to change this situation in any significant way. The GDP may grow, the state economic potential may increase, but the problem of poverty threatens to remain as topical and acute as before. On the one hand, it will restrain development of domestic market and thus national economic growth. Poverty conservation may also result in sharpening of social contradictions, especially because the unemployment problem becomes more topical. On the other hand, poverty conservation is an indispensable condition for maintaining China's high competitiveness in the world market.

Without any exaggeration it may be stated that the strategy of global economic offensive aimed at transforming China into the most economically powerful nation in the world is unable to solve the sharpest social problems domestically. At the same time even a partial success of this strategy may change the whole system of international economic relations in the most unpredictable way.

NOTES

1 "Zhou chuzhyu" kaifan janglue yui anle yanzhu, E 9.
2 Ma Weygand and Ma Weijie, *Zhungo: sya i gue u shi nyan. Guanjun yui menxian* [Glory and dreams. China in the next 50 years], (Haikou: Nankai chubanshe, 2000), E 72–79.
3 WCBF is a respectable Chinese organization whose everyday activity is managed by the secretariat. Participation in its bi-annual congresses is highly valued by most notable persons of Chinese emigration and top leaders of countries where such congresses are held. Such congresses deal with the analysis of international economic situation and work out economic recommendations for Chinese businessmen all over the world. The Forum was created by Singapore's Prime Minister Lee Kuan Yew, one of the most popular and successful politicians in the twentieth century.
4 "Modern tendencies of development of regional economic cooperation in Eastern Asia", *Proceedings of the scientific conference* (Moscow: Institute of World Economy and International Relations RAS, 2003), p. 45.
5 *Zhungo guangchandan dy shi u zhi zhuango daibyao dahoi weijyan hoipyan* [Collected documents of XV All-China congress of Communist Party of China] (Beijing: Jenming chubanshe, 1997), E 23, 29–30.
6 Ibid., pp. 312–13.
7 Jiang Zeming, *About the socialism with Chinese specificity*, p. 317.
8 "Zhou chuzhyu" kaifan janglue yui anle yanzhu, E 9.
9 Ibid.
10 Ma Weygand, Ma Weijie. Zhungo: sya i gue u shi nyan, E 178.
11 Ibid.
12 *Beijing syandai san bao*, 15 July 2002.
13 http://drcnet.com.cn/html_document/guoyan.../129594.
14 Ibid.
15 Ibid.
16 http://drcnet.com.cn/html_document/guoyan/gybd/2002-09-19/127603drcnetchetechdfgdghdaA023.asp.
17 Ibid.
18 Zhun Minzhun, "Zhungo zhie 'zhou chujue' dy yui zhun moshi", *Mosyke huashan bao*, 9 April 2003.
19 "Zhou chuzhyu" kaifan janglue yui anle yanzhu, E 15–16.
20 http://china.com.cn/chinese/2005/Mar/803635.htm.
21 Ibid.
22 Ibid., E 68–69.

23   Statement by Dai Xianglong, Governor of the People's Bank of China, at the sixth meeting of the International monetary and financial committee, www.pbc.gov.cn, (28 September 2002).

24   Statement by Zhou Xiaochuan, Governor of the People's Bank of China, International monetary and financial committee, www.pbc.gov.cn, (21 September 2003).

25   The course of negotiations in WTO Kankun summit has demonstrated that the most dynamically developing countries are already able to represent unified front as a counterbalance for developed countries. See A. Koksharov, "Globalization slows down", *Expert*, #35 (388), (2003: 40–44).

26   Statement by Zhou Xiaochuan, Governor of the People's Bank of China, International monetary and financial committee, www.imf.org, (21 September 2003).

27   See "Hearings in USA Senate Bank Committee", *Chinese currency manipulation*, www.manufacturersalliance.org, (1 May 2002).

28   "US blaming of yuan misplaced", http://drcnet.com.cn, (3 September 2003).

29   Especially sharp CPR's aversion is caused by the Code of corporative behaviour and international business accounting standards (GAAH).

30   "Governor Zhou Xiaochuan attended the fourth BIS Asian consultative council meeting and special governor's meeting in Sydney", www.pbc.gov.cn, (10 February 2003).

31   See "China monetary police report, 2004", www.pbc.gov.cn, (5 February 2005).

32   Ibid.

33   DeMeritt K., "China's tripling gold demand", www.worldnetdaily.com, (23 September 2004).

34   Ibid.

4
ASEAN and East Asia

Victor Sumsky

Since the second half of the 1960s and almost till the end of the 1990s East Asia was viewed by the world as a place where one economic miracle was followed by another, where countries considered eternally backward were successfully trying to catch up with the West, and economic dynamism, coupled with stable political foundations, was contributing to greater regional harmony. The impression that enterprising Asians would never let their luck slip away was badly shattered by the financial crisis of 1997–98. The same media outlets, research institutions and rating agencies that used to praise them, suddenly "saw the light" and started complaining as one about the flaws of "crony capitalism" — the system promoting alliances between bureaucracy and big business, rendering fair competition impossible and inseparable from paternalism, corruption and managerial mistakes.

Today passions induced by the crisis have largely settled down. Since the majority of the victims have improved their economic performance and China, untouched by the financial havoc of the late 1990s, continues to grow with an amazing speed, some observers tend to think that the Asian crisis is a thing of the past. That may be true if one views it as a period of dangerous unsteadiness for a number of national currencies and banking systems. But if one assumes that overcoming a serious crisis means getting over a set of its negative consequences — not just economic, but social and psychological, and those belonging to realms of ideology, domestic and international politics too — then the impression may be wrong. Among the factors prompting one to observe the East Asian scene with a degree of scepticism are the problems of individual ASEAN member countries and of this body as a whole. Many of these problems are determined by the differences between that global political environment in which the Association of Southeast Asian nations was born and matured, and the one emerging during the last decade.

COLD WAR BENEFICIARIES

Stating that East Asia has no regional structures of the European type and nothing like NATO to legitimize the U.S. military and political role on a far away continent, it is important to register the reasons why. An early attempt to put up such a military bloc was undertaken in 1954, with the creation of SEATO. The experiment disappointed even the staunchest Asian allies of the United States. With the escalation of the Indochina war in the 1960s those regional leaders who believed that the numerous problems of Southeast Asia were only aggravated by external intrusions, found plenty of evidence to confirm their views.[1]

On the other hand, the prospect of defeat in Vietnam was compelling the Americans to acknowledge that fighting communism with reliance on marionettes was a futile exercise. The emergence of ASEAN (1967) and the announcement of Richard Nixon's Guam Doctrine (1969) testified to a degree of mutual understanding concerning the desired regional order. By its very composition the original ASEAN-5 emphasized the quest of these nations for more independence in international affairs. The official statements of the Association showed preference for economic and cultural, not military cooperation. Although these traits could provoke some analogies with the theory and practice of non-alignment, the Americans did not worry about this too much. Wishing to disengage from the conflict in Indochina without provoking the spread of "the red menace" across the region, they needed a barrier on its way — a chain of viable political regimes sympathetic to each other and basically friendly towards the United States.

Implacable anti-communism, typical of the ASEAN rulers, happened to be an essential but not the only prerequisite of this project's implementation. The mutual complementarity of the elites was determined by a deeper semblance of political, economic and ideological aspirations. A model of capitalist modernization (or, one might say, of defeating communism) evolving in each of the five countries after the 1965 coup in Indonesia could be reduced, with an inevitable degree of simplification, to the following three features. First, guarantees of political stability were provided by rightist authoritarian regimes, some of them more, some less repressive and rigid.

Second, production and services were developing in the framework of export-oriented, mixed economies, combining market freedoms with a healthy dose of state regulation. Third, the realm of ideology was dominated by official nationalism, with no patience for leftist ideas but enough moderation and flexibility not to alienate foreign investors.

Impressive economic growth that lasted for almost three decades (with the notable exception of the Philippines in the 1980s and some minor interruptions in other cases) is often viewed as a primary result of the strategy chosen by the original ASEAN members. No less important, however, was the transformation of a number of states into viable subjects of history, to the point that national statehood itself was becoming somewhat stronger in Southeast Asia. Characteristically, this process was not at all detrimental to ASEAN as a regional body. In the words of Alexey Bogaturov, East Asian regionalism in general and ASEAN as its specific expression "emerged as a means of affirming the national self". Having realized their weaknesses in the mid-1960s, five Southeast Asian nations "embraced the idea of asserting the national self of each of them by joining their efforts. This line of thinking, however, was very far from the idea of trans-nationalism. While the European integration was suggesting the gradual elimination of state borders, the East Asian one was aimed at their reinforcement and painstaking mutual 'grinding-in' of the nations in order to avoid future quarrels that may reduce their capabilities. In other words, the Europeans were building a community, while the states of East Asia were just joining forces".[2]

Be it as it may, in the late 1980s and the early 1990s the ASEAN members seemed to be in such a shape that one could easily classify them — along with Japan, the first generation NICs and China — as major economic beneficiaries of the Cold War. Probably no one else understood it better than themselves and their American partners. Getting ever more jealous about the progress of East Asian "dragons" and "tigers", Washington was trying to convert its political and military triumph over the USSR into economic advantages, comparable in scope to that geopolitical achievement.

"BENEVOLENT HEGEMON" AND GEO-ECONOMIC PRIORITIES

As the Cold War was coming to its end, a sense of newly emerging challenges was growing up in the ASEAN capitals. For many years members of the Association were closing their ranks by working out and defending a joint position on the conflict in Cambodia. With subsiding rivalry between Moscow and Washington and normalization of Soviet–Chinese relations (as well as due to ASEAN's own diplomatic maneuvers), realistic possibilities for peace in Indochina were created and utilized. At the same time, this long-awaited shift was compelling the ASEAN members to look for new strategic objectives — as well as for new potential threats to regional peace and order — to justify their togetherness.

For quite a while the importance of the Cambodian conflict seemed so overwhelming that it "eclipsed" all other disagreements in Southeast Asia — including multilateral disputes over the island territories in the South China Sea (presumably possessing huge reserves of oil and natural gas). Chances that these "postponed" disputes would become hotter were now growing — not to speak of a set of bilateral problems capable of souring relations between several ASEAN members.

Above all, they suspected that without "the Soviet threat" the United States would lack a reason to maintain its military presence in Southeast Asia, if not in the whole of East Asian area. Closely linked to these suspicions were fears of a regional "power vacuum" and attempts to fill it by such powers as Japan and China, no longer comprising an anti-Soviet quasi-alliance with the United States. Although during the Cold War the ASEAN nations were actually following the lead of this threesome, they looked at each of the three with a sense of ambivalence.

Respecting Japan's economic achievements, counting on its capitals and seeking its technologies, members of ASEAN were viewing it as a nation that had not fully exorcized expansionist ambitions and was capable of redeveloping them if external limitations (namely, the U.S.–Japanese alliance) somehow slacken.

China fascinated Southeast Asians by unorthodox and productive approaches to socio-economic reform, by high competitiveness on world markets and the prospect of becoming a top player in the twenty-first century global economy. But admiration was giving place to apprehension at the thought that China, not tightly embraced by the United States and no longer at loggerheads with Russia, was now more free to pursue a great-power course in Southeast Asia at the expense of others.

The American manner to impose its own humanitarian and political standards on the rest of the world was provoking more and more allergic reactions around the region. There was also a general impression that, having adopted in the 1980s the Australian idea of creating a structure to promote economic integration and trade in the whole of the Asia-Pacific region, Washington was wishing to secure its leadership and its rules of the game inside the newly emerging body. In particular, such was the opinion of Dr Mahathir Mohamad, Prime Minister of Malaysia who made a counterproposal in 1990 to convene the East Asian Economic Caucus (EAEC) without the United States, Canada, Australia and New Zealand.[3]

Nevertheless, of all the possible regional hegemons, America was considered to be the most "benevolent" one. Its role was seen as indispensable for the stability in the region (to the point that when in 1991 the Senate of the Philippines took a stand that led to the evacuation of the U.S. bases from the archipelago, the American Navy and Air Force were immediately given access to seaports and air fields in the neighboring countries — though not in the framework of permanent basing). In all probability, the desire to retain the U.S. presence strongly motivated the ASEAN countries when in 1989 they joined the Asia-Pacific Economic Cooperation (APEC) forum and when four years later the American program of energizing APEC was approved at the summit in Seattle (in the expressive absence of the Malaysian Premier).

Anyway, at that point ASEAN self-confidence acquired in the process of longtime and steady economic growth was still with it. Preparing for the launching of APEC, the Association managed to position itself in such a way that the fate of the whole project became dependent on its collective approval. Joining a bigger integration scheme, it was providing itself with an additional incentive for internal consolidation, because otherwise its members would have not been able to talk on more or less equal terms to a set of powerful partners. Characteristically, right at the time of the APEC-inspired PR boom a number of plans to deepen and diversify intra-ASEAN ties — from "triangles of growth" concepts to proposals about switching to free trade — were advertised with equal enthusiasm.

When by the middle of the 1990s it became clear that a multilateral dialogue on problems of Asian and Pacific security was a must, ASEAN had both the prestige to take the initiative in its hands and the skill to use the advantages of the first move. The biggest of them was the right to determine the dialogue procedure in accordance with the established "ASEAN way". Its proponents saw no need to restrict discussions by protocol formalities or strive for a quick adoption of binding decisions. Instead they would opt for a gradual, step-by-step kind of natural emergence of a consensus. These were the principles and approaches that the ASEAN Regional Forum (ARF) tried to put into practice since 1994. Focused on the regional security issues, this mechanism itself looked like a natural outgrowth of consultations with extra-regional partners that ASEAN foreign ministers used to hold after their annual conferences.[4]

At the same time the Association (that had already expanded in 1984 by admitting Brunei) was putting into practice its old intentions to incorporate all Southeast Asian countries. In 1995 the ASEAN founders affiliated their former Indochina adversary — Vietnam, and did so in spite of remaining ideological differences. The summer of 1997 was marked by the admittance of Laos and Myanmar, and no one doubted that the admittance of Cambodia (already planned but postponed because of clashes among its rulers) was a matter of the near future. Apart from other reasons, this operation was undertaken to build up the political weight of ASEAN as it was claiming a special role inside APEC and tried to develop its external contacts — more intensive and diverse than ever before.[5]

The first Asia-Europe Meeting (ASEM) held in May 1996 in Bangkok became a graphic illustration of the latter tendency. The European Union members represented the Old World, while the members of ASEAN plus China, Japan and South Korea represented Asia. From the outsider's point of view it looked as if the participants wanted to figure out if there was anything they could have done together without permissions from the superpower, not belonging geographically to either Europe or Asia but being "the benevolent hegemon" of both continents. Naturally, this was a far cry from a display of militant anti-Americanism or an attempt to design a common strategy versus the United States. But even so, the dislike of *uncontrolled* American dominance over the globe — along with the interest in direct contacts and the willingness to take a position of greater flexibility in world affairs — was palpable in the postures of both Europeans and Asians.[6]

These interrelated, well thought out, at times even graceful maneuvers would have been neither possible, nor justified in the absence of the economic upsurge that Southeast Asia lived through in the early 1990s — the upsurge that these maneuvers were actually supposed to sustain. Observing the changes of that period in Southeast and East Asia, Russian experts were emphasizing the new quality of interregional interactions. According to Gennady Chufrin, the region was essentially moving "from one paradigm in development of international relations based on concepts and principles of geopolitics to a different one based on the principles of geo-economics". The geopolitical paradigm, he explained, was built around the primacy of national interests equated with inviolability of state borders, high defense capacity, and resistance to meddling in one's own domestic affairs, with a heavy accent on identifying national security challenges, potential adversaries and so on. By contrast, the geo-economic paradigm was placing emphasis on "securing high economic growth rates through internationalization of economic linkages". This new paradigm was tolerating "the washing out of national borders for the sake of free movement of goods, capital, labor force and technologies", prompting its adepts not so much to look around for existing external threats, as to prevent their growth through peaceful dialogue and agreements.[7]

Seeing the situation in a somewhat similar way, Alexey Bogaturov wrote about the "economic dominant" in regional interactions and concluded that since the end of the U.S.–Soviet rivalry there was no "visible increase in military activities" in East Asia. To be sure, right on the eve of the 1997–98 crisis that same author made a very timely remark that "economization of international relations" could only take place and acquire so much strength in the 1970s and 1980s "with the high degree of international stability reached and consolidated due to the bipolar confrontation between the USSR and the USA". But these reflections were leading him to a statement that "the breaking of the bipolar world structure" had no such negative impact on East Asia as on Europe, and "on the whole the preconditions for a stable development of the situation in the Asia-Pacific region are quite solid".[8]

GLOBALIZATION AND THE CREEPING COMEBACK OF GEOPOLITICS

Who but the United States as represented by its administration, political, and business elites should have been working hardest for the triumph of the geo-economic paradigm on the eve of the New Millennium? Had not these very forces done their best to secure the replacement of the Cold War era by the Brave New World of globalization — the world where new information technologies would open new horizons for the human race and the idea of global integration through modern electronic links and rational management would become the order of the day? Had not the preachers of the Washington Consensus — top leaders of the United States, international financial institutions and transnational corporations — stood up for market freedoms with all the unprecedented prosperity they would bring, for the free movement of goods, capitals and workers across the planet and for the quick abolition of anything impeding this wonderful change? Had not the United States laid down this agenda for APEC, and was not the latter working for East Asia's further "economization"?

A widely held opinion that Americans contemplate the future of East Asia and their own role in shaping it in the framework of the geo-economic paradigm was a major element of their "benevolent hegemon" image. The fact that the level of the U.S. military presence in the region had not gone down in any real sense and Washington's bilateral alliances with Tokyo and Seoul were left intact did not disturb the members of ASEAN: in their traditional view, "a power vacuum" would be sufficiently worse. Perhaps, it was easier for them to put up with the U.S. military supremacy because, in the words of Bogaturov, the end of the Cold War had given the United States the appearance of an "unintentional hegemon": its dominant position in the Asia-Pacific "turned out to be not so much the result of an increase in its military-political efforts, but as a consequence of inability… of Washington's potential rivals to counterbalance American might".[9]

Time was proving, however, that the status of "the only superpower" was a rather dubious gift of history. At its heart of hearts the U.S. power elite surely knew that this status could not be enjoyed forever. Nevertheless, for American patriots this fact of life should have been ruthlessly insulting, especially after all the mammoth efforts for the sake of victory in the Cold War and in a moment of hard-won triumph. Reminders about the need to avoid "an imperial overstretch" that would exhaust the U.S. capabilities had become commonplace in American political literature, but adequate steps in that direction were still lacking. Why? Maybe, because of the temptation to refashion old anti-Soviet alliances in such a way, that they would help to nip in the bud any future attempt to challenge the American hegemony, irrespective of who would be the challenger? To all appearance, that was exactly the story, although it seemed that even supporters of that line could not avoid second thoughts about its needlessly provocative and counter-productive character.

The impact of that line's implementation on East Asian affairs was anything but encouraging. In the 1990s Washington's position was not just unhelpful in terms of extinguishing the old hotbeds of tension on the Korean Peninsular and in the Taiwan Straits, but assured their fomentation. The consequences of such policies helped, in their turn, to justify attempts at drawing Japan, South Korea, and Taiwan into the construction of East Asian Theater Missile Defense under the U.S. aegis.[10] These efforts were coupled with the perception of the PRC as a state that was grooming itself for a geopolitical competition with the United States. Assessments of that type, widely circulating among the neo-conservative Reaganites, obviously influenced the treatment of Beijing by the Clinton administration — the treatment not well adjusted, liable to variations and getting on the nerves of a growing number of East Asians.[11]

At the same time, their own intentions and moves were arousing more and more displeasure in the United States. The expectations that APEC would work as a tool for opening up East Asian economies were proving futile. America's free trade offensive, launched at the APEC summits in Seattle (1993) and Bogor (1994), slowed down in Osaka (1995), where the Japanese, the representatives of ASEAN and other Asian participants managed to insist that they would determine themselves the tempo of external trade liberalization.[12] With their wish to add discussions of international security issues to the APEC mandate (and thus to steal the initiative from ARF), the Americans ran into resistance too. Those unhappy with the ASEM summit as an indirect challenge to Washington were irritated still more by ASEAN acceptance of Myanmar, whose military rulers were portrayed in the West as the worst human rights violators. Public reprimands for the same humanitarian reasons, especially for the mistreatment of East Timor, were periodically given to Jakarta. The informal but acknowledged leader of ASEAN did not miss a chance to return the favour. In 1997, months before its financial collapse, the New Order regime pointedly refused to buy a squadron of F-16 fighter planes, announcing instead the purchase of Russian military equipment (including twelve SU-30s). From the U.S. point of view, this was a bold move fortifying a dangerous trend. Just two years before, in 1995, Kuala Lumpur came to an agreement with Moscow concerning the supply of eighteen MIG-29 fighter jets, and did so in spite of American arm-twisting. Following Malaysia's example, not just Indonesia but Thailand and the Philippines were taking keen interest in military-technical cooperation with Russia.[13]

In Bogaturov's terms, a sequence of these situations could be viewed as a manifestation of "regional space compression" — in other words, as a sign of the small and medium East Asian countries' growing importance (approved in the Cold War environment by America itself, but now beginning to irk "the only superpower").[14] It seems, however, that unusually frequent disagreements between the United States and the ASEAN countries could be explained in some other ways. America's anti-statist, trans-nationalist and pro-market interpretation of globalization was hardly compatible in its radicalism with anything else — and surely not with the intentions to strengthen national statehood in the ASEAN member countries. In practice they were told to dismantle the model of development that had shown its efficiency and to do it at the time when none of them had completed a national integration project. No wonder that these countries were not just refusing to obey, but tried to justify their choice through the concept of Asian values. The latter was presented to the world as a kind of common doctrine explaining the specifics of modernizing efforts in Southeast and East Asia.[15]

Year after year all sorts of not quite harmless contradictions were being accumulated in East Asia, laying ground for what might be termed as the comeback of geopolitics. In the mid-1990s booming capital markets and massive foreign investments provided a smokescreen to cover that perspective. But this same boom — an outcome of hasty financial liberalization in several East Asian countries — became a prologue to a blow delivered by transnational currency speculators not just against some national economies but against the region as a political and economic entity.

ASEAN KNOCKED-DOWN

The strictly economic preconditions and manifestations of the crisis that started on 2 July 1997 with the crash of the Thai baht have been described in considerable detail.[16] Without retelling that story, let us turn to the immediate political consequences of the 1997–98 financial upheaval that meant so much for ASEAN as a whole.

To begin with, the crisis hit the Association at the moment when, having embraced all the countries of the region (minus Cambodia that got its membership card in 1999) it acquired a host of new problems. Adapting the newcomers to the traditions and norms of collective behaviour that had evolved over the years was not easy — especially with the differences between them and the "old-timers" in terms of socio-economic development, types of political regimes and official doctrines. Never before had ASEAN inner heterogeneity reached these levels, and managing (let alone solving) this problem was still harder in the midst of the crisis.

In theory, the negative aspects of ASEAN quick enlargement could have been partly neutralized by the confident leadership of one of the member countries. To ASEAN's great misfortune, Indonesia that was always seen as "the first among equals" in the Association, became a primary victim of the financial storm. After rupiah devaluation and the collapse of the stock market in the late 1997 to early 1998 it had to go through a paralysis of the banking system, drastic production declines and mass layoffs among industrial workers, shortages of essential commodities, accompanied by ethnic and religious clashes, the biggest anti-Chinese riots in the history of Jakarta and demonstrations of students demanding instant democratization.

In May 1998 General Suharto who had ruled the country since the late 1960s was removed from presidency, but that was only the start of a new phase of trials. The society seemed incapable of either establishing "a working democracy" or getting back to "constructive authoritarianism". Tensions between the center and the regions — especially such provinces as East Timor (that had come under the UN administration in late 1999 and was proclaimed an independent state in May 2002),[17] Aceh and Irian Jaya — felt more and more menacing, prompting parallels with the break-ups of the Soviet Union and Yugoslavia.[18] The prospect of the archipelago's "balkanization", with the consequent exodus of refugees, distortions of fragile inter-ethnic balances in the neighbouring countries and destabilization of the whole of Southeast Asia were now discussed not only by journalists, but by officials too.[19] Even in the estimates of those who were not prone to alarmism, Indonesia's "calming down" was supposed to take about a decade.

One could only guess how this period of protracted instability might affect ASEAN and if the latter was capable of doing anything at all to alleviate the pains of the wounded giant.[20]

In fact, the whole philosophy of intra-ASEAN political behaviour was undergoing a severe test. Michael Leifer who had been watching the Association since the moment of its inception with unmatched degree of competence, wrote in 1995 that this body was demonstrating not so much the capacity to solve problems, as the skill to deal with them in a delicate way and to create "the milieu in which they either do not arise or can be readily managed".[21] Less than two years after ASEAN became engulfed by problems calling for comprehensive, energetic and urgent solutions. The titles of the documents adopted in December 1998 at the sixth ASEAN summit in Vietnam — Hanoi Plan of Action and Statement on Bold Measures — suggested awareness of that fact and readiness for creative, pro-active moves. But moves considered "bold" by the pre-crisis standards (like the acceleration of ASEAN Free Trade Area arrangements or initiatives to enhance the ASEAN investment climate) were a far cry from what was needed to reinvigorate the group.[22]

Pessimistic observations concerning ASEAN future were prompted by disagreements among the member-states about the nature of the crisis and the absence of a coordinated anti-crisis strategy.[23] Roughly speaking, some thought that lack of genuine market freedom was the source of all the troubles, while others abhorred the chaos of unregulated markets. The first position meant that the sick national economies should be cured through greater involvement with the globalizing/liberalizing world economy, while the second emphasized the need for protection against excesses of globalization. Among the proponents of "bolder liberal solutions" were the leaders of Brunei, the Philippines, Singapore, IMF-assisted Thailand, and Indonesia (the latter probably with some reservations). Firmly on the side of "guided liberal economy" stood Malaysia (where currency controls introduced in September 1998 stabilized ringgit exchange rate and created a base for the quick resumption of economic growth).[24] Vietnam, Laos, and Myanmar basically shared this approach. But irrespective of who was right and who was wrong in this debate, the obvious looser was ASEAN, unable to speak with a single voice and act as one in a moment of trial.

Last but not least, as mentioned earlier, for three decades a more or less the same model of modernization had been a major precondition of the ASEAN members' mutual compatibility. By discrediting this model, the 1997–98 crisis was shattering not just individual states and economies, but regional cooperation structures that were embracing them.

THE GAINS AND THE LOSSES OF THE ONLY SUPERPOWER

To America this crisis, at least initially, had come as a reward for the discomforts of "regional space compression". Failing to draw East Asia into the Anglo-Saxon operating mode through the mechanism of APEC, the United States pursued the same objective in the crisis period by relying on the IMF — and not unsuccessfully. Although the IMF's "assistance" came along with a set of painful conditions (like limits on budgetary expenses, mass bankruptcies of insolvent companies and admittance of foreign investors to segments of domestic markets previously inaccessible to them), the leaders of Thailand, Indonesia, and South Korea had to accept it under the pressing circumstances.[25]

The fact that the crisis was weakening not just ASEAN, but new forums for promotion of regional security (ARF) and multilateral cooperation (ASEM) was hardly upsetting for Washington. Not enjoying a deciding vote in ARF and being a non-participant in ASEM, it did not have much to loose in either of these cases.[26] Seizing the opportunity, the United States offered bigger military aid to impoverished Southeast Asians in exchange for greater access to their naval and air facilities, training grounds and maintenance centers. These initiatives were clearly supposed to add new dimensions to American military presence and to shorten "the strategic lead" on which the United States was holding its regional partners.[27]

But while making these gains Washington was undermining its own reputation in the eyes of the crisis victims. The latter were becoming highly dissatisfied with the IMF stabilization programs, and for good reasons. First, implementation of such programs was invariably resulting (and, judging by the Fund's history, could not help but result) in further worsening of the situations that had originally forced the borrowers to appeal to the creditor of last resort.[28] Second, there were indications that the United States and the IMF were trying not so much to help the economies of the region as to bail out some influential foreign investors who faced the prospect of incurring heavy losses in East Asia. Third, the kind of restructuring prescribed by IMF might easily end up with the dirt-cheap sale of the best local banks and production facilities to transnational dealers, depriving the ASEAN states of the ability to pursue independent economic policies.[29]

On top of that, the Clinton administration blocked the initiative of Japan and Taiwan to create the AMF (designed to assist the crisis victims without the typical IMF conditions), employed the IMF, according to the confessions of its former boss Michael Camdessus, for purposes of Suharto's deposition, and, in the person of Vice-President Albert Gore (who represented the United States at the APEC summit in Kuala Lumpur in November 1998), openly urged Malaysians to disobey their duly constituted government that had had the temerity to reject the IMF prescriptions.[30]

"10+3"

Painful as it was, the trauma of the Asian crisis had not reduced the ASEAN leaders to fatalism. Signs of the search for a way out were already visible in December 1997: right after the ASEAN summit that had been held in the Malaysian capital, its participants were joined by counterparts from China, Japan and South Korea. Next year a similar session took place in Hanoi. In 1999 the same group issued in Manila its Joint Statement on Cooperation in East Asia. Soon after that, during a conference in Singapore in 2000 it expressed a wish to create a regional free trade area. Although the meetings of these players were outwardly focused on issues of multilateral economic cooperation, some decisions (like the one taken in May 2000 in Chiang Mai to set up a system of bilateral currency swap arrangements that would decrease the participants' dependence on the IMF favours) had clear political implications. In fact, the whole of the "ASEAN+3" or "10+3" process, as it has been called since the late 1990s, was loaded with discernible political meanings, to the point that even top officials involved in its launching would not miss a chance to emphasize this (like Syed Hamid Albar, Malaysia's Foreign Minister who warmly welcomed ASEAN+3 as the reincarnation of the East Asian Economic Caucus idea — knowing all too well that Stanley Roth, the U.S. Assistant Secretary of State for East Asia and the Pacific, had been proclaiming that idea dead).[31]

For East Asians, an instinctive wish to distance themselves from the United States after the events of 1997–98 would have been more than understandable. But cautious and pragmatic representatives of ASEAN (just like those of China, Japan, and South Korea) would have never dragged themselves into a conflict with America for purely emotional reasons. Above anything else, their maneuvers were prompted by a sober assessment of what was going on.

Presumably, losing Indonesia as its strong inner core and realizing the essence of the U.S. position, ASEAN felt the need to neutralize these unhappy trends by forming external partnerships of a rather special kind. Such partnerships, helping to overcome the crisis and to prevent its recurrences, had to contain an element of challenge that would not allow the ASEAN members to turn away from each other and "relax". In the late 1990s economic heavyweights of Northeast Asia — China, Japan, and South Korea — looked like the best candidates for involvement in such interactions. The first one displayed immunity to stock and currency exchange fevers and in the midst of the crisis refrained from devaluating yuan, earning the gratitude of the neighbours. The second one, in spite of its lengthy economic stagnation and failure to form the AMF, remained to ASEAN a major source of financial assistance and investments. The third one, incurring heavy losses in 1997, had already managed to accumulate so much productive capacity and was so active in the ASEAN area, that to neglect it would have been unwise.

On the diplomatic front, ASEAN was "courting" this trio in approximately the same fashion in which Malaysia, Singapore, Thailand, and the Philippines were "courting" Indonesia at the time of the Associations' birth. Back then Indonesia, in view of its territorial size, ambitions and development potential, was offered the role of the group's unofficial leader and the stage to play this role — under condition that the leadership will be non-aggressive, not hampering the rights and dignity of the followers.[32] Now, it seemed, somewhat similar offers were made by the ASEAN to Northeast Asian states — first and foremost to China and Japan. The presence of these two mammoth players (who disagreed quite often but looked destined for cooperation) in the "10+3" scheme opened significant opportunities for regulating the regional balance of forces. Staying one on one with any of them could have been less than comfortable for ASEAN. On the contrary, belonging to the same group with China and Japan would allow to appeal to the former in case of difficulties with the latter and vice-versa, or to mediate between them if they have a quarrel themselves, and to use the new forum to cover and smoothen the problems that would prevent the participants from achieving their major common goal. The latter, as it appeared, was tantamount to restoration of economic dynamism and political governability — both at the level of Southeast Asia as a whole and of the nations comprising it. Or, to put it in a different way, in placing back the priorities of geo-economics over those of geopolitics, as had been (or seemed to be) typical of Southeast Asia not too long ago.

If these collective aspirations are understood correctly, it is not hard to take a few steps more and make it clear why today, with all the traditional ambivalence about China to the South and to the East of its borders, it is widely accepted as a desirable partner. Isn't China a major force sustaining the economic growth in the region — and, by implication, its hopes for a brighter geo-economic future? And if so, then isn't China a natural aspirant to the position of East Asia's "benevolent hegemon", especially since this position is now all but vacant?[33]

QUESTIONS AND PROBLEMS

That said, it should be noted that the ASEAN+3 scheme does not consist of merits and pluses alone — especially from the ASEAN own point of view. In too many ways the outcome of this undertaking is not dependent upon the Association and its members. For example, can the present generation of the Japanese elite pull the country out of the economic stupor? Will the Chinese manage to minimize the rise of internal tensions that usually accompanies accelerated modernization and may result, due to even smallest blunders by political leadership, in a fearful social explosion? Will there be a unified Korea in the foreseeable future, and if yes, then how this unification will proceed? The answers are crucially important for the fate of new East Asian initiatives, but it is not ASEAN that will provide them.

On the other hand, the problems that the members of ASEAN must tackle themselves (and without whose solution the ASEAN+3 will not justify itself in their eyes) are too complicated to be solved soon. First and foremost, these are the national statehood crises — not just the ones that have been dragging on for decades in Cambodia and Myanmar, but also those that are evolving in the "old" ASEAN countries with extensive modernization experiences, notably Indonesia and the Philippines. And even where things look more promising, there is the need to readjust the ASEAN model of modernization to changing realities — for instance, through developing greater cooperation between the nation states and the growing civil societies.

Another long-term problem of ASEAN+3 is compatibility between the rising Big China (including the prosperous Chinese minorities of Southeast Asia) and the Islamic communities of the region, whose poor share of development fruits breeds a lot of bitterness — a factor not to be dismissed in discussions about the origins of local religious extremism.

In a short-term prospective, an overlapping of Japanese economic stagnation, South Korea's preoccupation with the North and China's continued upsurge spontaneously leads to a transformation of 10+3 into 10+1, standing for ASEAN plus China. Those who feel uneasy about this turn of things try to add another element to the equation — India that has become of late a regular participant in East Asian forums. While for some of the ASEAN members this is a welcome measure to counter China's growing prominence, Indonesia as ASEAN own traditional leader feels more and more eclipsed in the company of strong external partners — not a good sign for the future of either the Association or the bigger East Asian group.[34] On top of that, the prospect of American attempts to derail the East Asian initiative in a classical divide and rule fashion is also there. By classifying Myanmar as an "outpost of tyranny", Washington is laying ground for intensified pressure not just on that country, but on the whole of ASEAN (whose other members are not uncritical of Yangon home policies) and, incidentally, on China (whose military and economic help is of great importance to Myanmar's rulers).[35] Other indications of America's possible moves can be found in the recent publications of Francis Fukuyama.[36] This influential writer believes that the 6-party talks on Korean problems involving the United States, China, Japan, Russia, South Korea, and North Korea should be transformed into a permanent security body. Certain ASEAN members — but, characteristically, not all of them — may also be invited to come in at some point, explains Fukuyama. His denial of participation to ASEAN as a whole and his clear assumption that the ARF is not a useful venue for security discussions should neither be missed nor underestimated.

All in all, indications that ASEAN and East Asia have entered a period of serious uncertainty are multiplying. This period has just begun, and we have yet to understand its trends and contradictions.

NOTES

1   Acharya A., *The Quest for Identity: International Relations of Southeast Asia* (Oxford: 2000), pp. 63–68.

2   Bogaturov A.D., *Velikiye derzhavy na Tikhom okeane, Istoriya i teoriya mezhdunarodnykh otnosheniy v Vostochnoy Azii posle vtoroy mirovoy voyny (1945–1995)* [Great Powers on the Pacific: History and Theory of International Relations in East Asia after the Second World War, 1945–1995] (in Russian) (Moscow: 1997), pp. 201–202. Bogaturov's views are consonant with the ideas of Acharya concerning "the nationalist vision of regionalism" in Southeast Asia that started to form well before the emergence of ASEAN (Acharya, *The Quest for Identity*, pp. 43–51).

3   Mahathir M. and Ishihara S., *The Voice of Asia: Two Leaders Discuss the Coming Century*, (Tokyo: 1995), pp. 26–31, 42–49.

4   Acharya, *The Quest for Identity*, pp. 143–48.

5   Maletin N.P., "Ot ASEAN-6 k ASEAN-10: novyi geopoliticheskiy factor v ATR" [From ASEAN-6 to ASEAN-10: New Geopolitical Factor in the Asia Pacific Region], *ASEAN i vedushchiye strany ATR: problemy i perspectivy* [ASEAN and the Leading Countries of the Asia Pacific Region: Problems and Prospects] (in Russian) (Moscow: 2002).

6   Vatikiotis M. and Islam S., "A Whole New Game: Asia — European Meeting Seems to Recast Relations", *Far Eastern Economic Review* (hereafter cited as *FEER*), (Hong Kong), 14 March 1996, p. 17.

7   Chufrin G.I., "Yugo-Vostochnaya Aziya: ot geopolitiki k geoekonomike" [Southeast Asia: From Geopolitics to Geoeconomics], *Strany Yugo-Vostochnoy Azii na rubezhe XXI veka: traditsii i sovremennost, problemy politicheskoy i ekonomicheskoy integratsii* [Southeast Asian Countries on the Threshold of the 21st Century: Traditions and Modernity, Problems of Political and Economic Integration] (in Russian) (Moscow: 1994), p. 15.

8   Bogaturov A.D., *Velikiye derzhavy na Tikhom okeane*, pp. 213–18.

9   Ibid., p. 255.

10 Bernstein R. and Munro R.H., *The Coming Conflict with China* (New York: 1997), pp. 182–83.

11 Lutterbeck D. and Gilley B., Sherry A., "Riders on the Storm", *FEER*, 25 June 1998, pp. 10–12.

12 Bello W., *The Resubordination of East Asia*, (Part 1), http://www.inq7.net.opi/2002/jun/14/text/opiwbello-1-p.htm.

13 Litovkin D., "Dorogu indoneziyskim SU prolozhili malayziyskiye MIGi" [The way for SUs to be sold to Indonesia was prepared by the MIGs sold to Malaysia], *Izvestiya*, (Moscow: 7 August 1997, in Russian); Kosyrev D., "V Moskvu priyezzhayet potentsialnyi pokupatel rossiyskikh istrebiteley" [A Potential Buyer of Russian Fighter Planes Comes to Moscow], *Nezavisinaya Gazeta* (in Russian) (Moscow: 10 September 1997); Korotchenko I., "Moskva predlagayet oruzhiye Bangkoku" [Moscow Offers Weapons to Bangkok], *Nezavisinaya Gazeta*, 24 October 1997; Bickers C., "Bear Market: Russia Wants to Be Top Arms Supplier to Asia", *FEER*, 4 September 1997, pp. 25–26.

14 Bogaturov's concept of "regional space compression" is elaborated in the closing chapters of his fundamental monograph (Bogaturov, *Velikiye derzhavy na Tikhom okeane*, Part 4).

15 See, for example: Kausikan B., "Asia's Different Standard", *Foreign Policy*, no. 92 (Washington, D.C.: 1993); see also: Acharya, *The Quest for Identity*, pp. 138–42.

16 See, for example: Minayev S.V., "Vostochnoaziatskiy finansovyi krizis" [East Asian Financial Crisis], *Vostochnaya Aziya na poroge XXI veka* [East Asia on the Threshold of the 21st Century] (in Russian) (Moscow: 2000); Montes M.F. and Popov V.V., *"Aziatskiy virus" ili "gollandskaya bolezn"? Teoriya i istoriya valyutnykh krizisov v Rossii i drugikh stranakh* ["Asian Virus" or "Dutch Desease"? Theory and History of Currency Crises in Russia and Other countries] (in Russian) (Moscow: 1999); Johnson C., *Blowback: The Costs and Consequences of American Empire*, (New York: 2000, ch. 9); Stiglitz J.E., *Globalization and its Discontents* (New York: 2002, ch. 4); *The 1997 "Asia Crisis"*, http://users.cyberone.com.au/myers/asia-crisis.html; *Tigers in Trouble: Financial Governance, Liberalisation and Crises in East Asia*, (London: 1998).

17 On the story of East Timor and its separation from Indonesia see: Urlyapov I.V., Urlyapov V.F., *Vostochnyi Timor: ternistyi put k nezavisimosti* [East Timor: A Thorny Path to Independence] (in Russian) (Moscow: 2005); *Out of the Ashes: Destruction and Reconstruction of East Timor*, (Adelaide: 2000).

18 Parallels between Indonesia shattered by the crisis and the Soviet Union on the eve of its collapse are drawn in a series of articles by S. Mitin and M. Yusin, published under the common title *Konets indoneziyskogo chuda* [The End of Indonesian Miracle] *Izvestiya*, (in Russian), 9–11 July 1998.

19 "Relax — a Little: Goh Says Paternalism Has its Limitations", *FEER*, 24 December 1998, p. 15; Richardson M., "Jakarta Jars Its Neighbors: Nearby Countries, Fearing a Rush of Refugees, Are Publicly Worrying About Indonesian Unrest", *International Herald Tribune*, (Paris), 9 December 1998.

20 Pereira D., " '8 Years' to Return to Normalcy", *Straits Times* (Singapore), 9 June 1998.

21 Leifer M., "The Issue in ASEAN", *FEER*, 30 November 1995, p. 34.

22 Torode G., "ASEAN: Discord Visible as Leaders Warn of Unchecked Globalization", *South China Morning Post* (hereafter cited as *SCMP*), (Hong Kong), 16 November 1998.

23 Richardson M., "Southeast Asia Fears Damage to its Influence: Leaders at ASEAN Summit Call for Rebuilding Unity Amid Region's Economic Woes", *International Herald Tribune*, 16 December 1998; Torode, "ASEAN: Call for Unity Fail to Dispel Sense of Crisis", *SCMP*, 17 December 1998.

24 Mohamad M., "Malaysia: Bouncing Back", *FEER*, 11 February 1999, p. 31. See also: Kosyrev, "Iskusstvo byt nepriyatnym. Doktor Mahathir Mohamad sozdal protsvetayushchuyu razvituyu stranu, spas yeyo ot aziatskogo krizisa i pobedil v spore s IMF" [The Art of Being Unpleasant: Dr. Mahathir Mohamad Has Created a Prosperous Developed Nation, Saved it from the Asian Crisis and Won in a Dispute with the IMF], *Doktor Mahathir Mohamad: politik i lichnost* [Dr. Mahathir Mohamad: The Politician and the Man] (in Russian) (Moscow: 2001).

25 Bello, *The Resubordination of East Asia*, (Part 1).

26 Bello, *The Resubordination of East Asia*, (Part 2), http://www.inq7.net.opi/2002/jun/19/text/opiwbello-1-p.htm.

27 Richardson, "In Asia, a New Mutual Defense: U.S. to Offer Aid in Return for Access to Local Bases", *International Herald Tribune*, 3 December 1998.

28 A classical analysis of real — as opposed to declared — objectives of the IMF was done way back in the 1970s by Cheryl Payer (see: Payer C., *The Debt Trap: The IMF and the Third World* (Harmondsworth: 1974). Among the later works upholding this tradition and based on East Asian material are the books of Robin Broad, Walden Bello and his co-authors (see: Broad R., *Unequal Alliance, 1979–86: The World Bank, the International Monetary Fund and the Philippines*, (London: 1988); Bello W., Cunningham S. and Poh L.K., *A Siamese Tragedy: Development and Desintegration in Thailand*, (London and New York: 1998,

ch. 3). Another highly recommended publication is the already mentioned *Globalization and its Discontents* by Joseph E. Stiglitz.

29 Bello, *The Resubordination of East Asia* (Part 1); Johnson, *Blowback*, pp. 207–210.

30 Hanke S., "Suharto, too, Was a Victim of Regime Change", *Australian*, (Melbourne: 29 April 2003); Johnson, *Blowback*, pp. 209–212.

31 "America's Asia Point Man: Roth Defends APEC, Engagement and Al Gore", *Asiaweek*, (Hong Kong), 19 February 1999; Oorjitham S., "ASEAN+3 = 'EAEC' ", Ibid., 15 March 2000; "Singapore Summit Could Signal 'End of American Empire in Asia' (Interview: Dr. Chalmers Johnson)", *Executive Intelligence Review* (Washington, D.C.), 8 December 2000, pp. 9–12.

32 Urlyapov V.F., *Indoneziya i mezhdunarodnyye otnosheniya v Aziatsko-Tikhookeanskom regione* [Indonesia and International Relations in the Asia Pacific Region] (in Russian) (Moscow: 1993), pp. 4–6; Leifer M., *Indonesia's Foreign Policy*, (London: 1983), pp. 120–21.

33 Mosyakov D.V., "Protsessy regionalnoy konsolidatsii v Vostochnoy i Yugo-Vostochnoy Azii i yapono-kitaiskiye otnosheniya" [Processes of Regional Consolidation in East and Southeast Asia and Japan-China Relations], *Yugo-Vostochnaya Aziya v 2001 g. Aktualnyye problemy razvitiya* [Southeast Asia in 2001: Urgent Problems of Development] (in Russian) (Moscow: 2002), pp. 55–57; Roy D., "China and Southeast Asia: ASEAN Makes the Best of the Inevitable", *Currents*, 10, (Honolulu: Summer 2003): 22–25.

34 Eric Teo Chu Cheow, "East Asia Summit's Birthing Pains", *Straits Times*, 22 February 2005.

35 Bremmer I., "Bush Signals a Revolution in Foreign Policy", *International Herald Tribune*, 29 January 2005.

36 Fukuyama F., "Re-Envisioning Asia", *Foreign Affairs* (New York: January/February 2005). A summary of this paper appeared in the *International Herald Tribune*, 10 December 2004, and an abbreviated Russian translation in *Dipkurier NG* (Moscow), 7 February 2005.

5

Regional Economic Cooperation in Northeast Asia: Issues and Prospects

Alexander Fedorovsky

Development of East Asian countries such as China, Japan, and the Republic of Korea (ROK) depends to a large degree on their multilateral economic cooperation in NorthEast Asia (NEA). Lately, especially in the second half of the 1990s, commercial, investment and technological exchanges between them grew up significantly both on the bilateral and multilateral levels. At the beginning of the first decade of the twenty-first century regional economic cooperation in NEA entered its new stage of development. New economic situation in China, Japan, and the ROK, latest trends in their foreign economic policies as well as a growing involvement of Japanese, Chinese, and South Korean companies in international business activities typical for the era of globalization were among most important factors influencing regional cooperation. Under these conditions economic relations between the three countries in fact deeply influenced the whole architecture of regional economic framework.

The emergence of NEA regional cooperation depended on several key factors. Thus, active consultations between Japan, China, and the ROK on many important regional issues came as a result of their reduced confidence in international economic organizations since the latter proved to be unable either to prevent the 1997–98 East Asian economic crisis or to minimize its consequences. Also constant disputes among WTO members paralysed the WTO modernization. According to the NEA countries the failure of negotiations in Cancun (Mexico) was bad news symbolizing the slow down of reforming international trade and of cooperation at the global level. As a result many countries decided to upgrade their economic structures as well as their foreign economic relations by improving regional economic cooperation. Japan, China, and the ROK were among them.

APEC IN CRISIS

There was growing skepticism among APEC members, including the NEA countries, regarding efficiency of APEC as an international economic organization. In fact APEC failed to initiate an anti-crisis policy in the second half of the 1990s and also failed to offer any assistance to the countries in need during the crisis. At the same time, it would be fair to note that APEC did not have any anti-crisis mechanisms. Therefore, this international organization was not prepared to work out and to implement practical anti-crisis measures. In fact APEC was established at the end of the 1990s primarily as an international institution for consultations and information exchanges between Pacific countries.

Some of the Pacific countries expected that it would be possible for them to solve their economic problems in APEC more successfully and within shorter time than in WTO.[1] But these hopes of APEC members have not been realized so far. According to the prevailing views the slowdown of trade liberalization was among the most important reason for the APEC crisis at the turn of the century.[2]

The main task of APEC was to help regional countries to adapt their economies to the challenges of globalization of the world economy. But it was often difficult to realize these goals because APEC was actually incapable to support positive and to neutralize negative regional economic trends. As a consequence doubts were spreading among Pacific countries regarding prospects of regional cooperation under the APEC model.

Some experts believed that among the most important problems was an absence of unity among APEC members on such key issues as APEC priorities and prospects of regional cooperation, as well as a low domestic support for APEC activities in Pacific countries. Others emphasized lack of interest among Pacific countries for a multinational cooperation in the Asia-Pacific region and dissatisfaction of the United States with APEC.[3]

In any case many developed as well as developing Pacific countries were dissatisfied with APEC as a regional institution and its ability to realize declared goals. As a result new legal and administration frameworks were required in order to stimulate development of regional economic cooperation. Under these circumstances negotiations on bilateral and sub-regional cooperation were resumed in the Pacific region. At the beginning of the new century Japan, China, and the ROK were the only countries in the region that were not members of any bilateral or sub-regional economic organizations. But since that time, the economic policies of these countries have changed and cooperation between China, Japan, and the ROK at the bilateral and triangular levels increased radically.

NEW STAGE OF ECONOMIC COOPERATION IN NEA

A new stage in development of regional economic relations in NEA began in October 1998. At that time South Korean President Kim Dae-jung and Japanese Prime Minister K. Obuchi reached an agreement to initiate bilateral long-term economic partnership. One of the results of that improvement in relations between Japan and South Korea became "Bilateral Investment Agreement" which was signed in March 2002. This agreement also influenced the overall situation in NEA because both Japan and the ROK considered it to be a model for institutionalization of regional economic relations. Thus, in the opinion of South Korean Ministry of Foreign Affairs this agreement became a starting point of economic integration in NEA.[4]

Explaining changes in Japan's foreign economic policy Minister of MITI, T. Hiranuma said in 2000 that the WTO could not keep pace with changes in the world economy.[5] Because Japan had to carry out deep structural reforms at home it was interested in promoting regional economic exchanges and in upholding activities of regional institutions.

H. Tanaka, Head of Bureau of international economic relations at Japan's Ministry of Foreign Affairs, noted that intensification of economic relations at the regional level should stimulate positive trends in Japan's structural policy. He underscored several basic conditions under which Japan would initiate a more active regional policy in NEA: 1) bilateral Free Trade Agreements (FTA) had to become important elements in the process of liberalization of global economy; 2) Japan would sign FTAs not only with the NEA countries but with other countries as well; 3) regionalism was to become an element of the globalization process. Also Japanese Federation of Economic Organizations (*Keidanren*) in its special report published in 2000 strongly recommended to the government to work out a long-term regional strategy.[6]

Many Japanese experts believed that Northeast Asian countries were faced with many common long-term problems which could not be overcome unilaterally even by a powerful state. According to Director of Nippon Institute of Research Advancement (NIRA), Professor T. Ceoya, energy and environment problems were among most prominent issues of regional cooperation in NEA.[7] At an official level an idea of sub-regional cooperation in energy was put forward by the Japanese Prime Minister Obuchi in 1998 during his visit to China.

Unprecedented long stagnation of Japan's economy was another factor influencing economic situation in NEA. Various problems negatively affected the Japanese economy in the 1990s and undermined an economic role of Japan in international relations in East Asia. But in spite of negative economic trends in Japan, economic ties between Japan and Northeast Asian countries, especially between Japan and China, Japan and the ROK were developing at a fast rate. Promoting ties with China and South Korea was particularly important for Japan because trade, investment, and technological cooperation with these countries stimulated modernization of the Japanese economy.

Several domestic as well as external economic and political reasons were behind the increase of interest of China and the ROK in promoting regional cooperation in NEA. Regional economic relations became especially important for them at the time when both countries were undergoing deep social and economic reforms. On the one hand, Beijing and Seoul had to open national economies to the outside world. On the other, a sort of a transitional period was necessary for both countries in order to adapt domestic industries and agriculture to the new global challenges. Regionalism was also to help them to adapt national economic institutions, legal systems and business structures to international standards at the era of globalization.

One the most important goals of economic reforms initiated in the Republic of Korea after the 1997–98 financial crisis was the radical restructuring of the Korean economy. This process was closely connected with diversification of external economic relations of the country. Promotion of trade and investment relations with China and Japan became a very important element of Korea's economic policy. Economic liberalization in South Korea meant transformation of national institutions in accordance with international standards and an adaptation of the South Korean economy to the process of globalization through cooperation with the WTO. At the same time, the ROK tried its best to use regionalism for these purposes.

As Professor Kim Cae-one of Seoul National University noted, "North East Asian markets are vitally important for South Korea's economic growth in the near and in the long-run perspective".[8] This point of view is widespread among South Korean experts. Besides many scholars in the ROK believe that economic integration between Japan, China and the ROK can help to overcome hard historical legacy in NEA and to prevent deterioration of political relations between the three countries.[9]

It is necessary to emphasize that international relations in NEA depend to a large extent on China's growing role as a regional power. One of the important consequences of a long and dynamic economic development of China and its transition to a market economy became a new balance of economic power in NEA. The huge, growing Chinese domestic market as well as a large-scale expansion of Chinese exports to the neighbouring markets had to be taken into account by governments and business groups in all of the NEA countries. Also, China's accession to the WTO created notable additional opportunities and challenges for regional economies.

During the 1990s, one of the main priorities of China's foreign economic policy was joining the WTO under the best possible conditions. Membership in the WTO was necessary for Beijing in order to help integration of the Chinese economy into the world economy and to simultaneously stimulate domestic market reforms. Growing competition at home, as a result of liberalization of China's foreign trade, had to support transformation of state-run enterprises into market-oriented institutions and at the same time to prevent the establishment of Chinese "oligarch business groups". Under membership in the WTO, the Chinese central and regional bureaucracy had little choice but to improve administrative, legal, and institutional conditions for modernization of China's economy. Meanwhile, since the end of the 1990s, Beijing began to pay more attention to international economic cooperation at the regional level. Since 1997 Beijing together with Tokyo and Seoul started to take part in ASEAN annual forums. Since 1999 China also started to participate in annual summits of the three Northeast Asian countries.

There are several important reasons for the intensification of China's foreign economic policy in NEA. First, expanding regional cooperation with such important economic partners as Japan and the ROK presents good opportunity for China to overcome negative consequences of globalization. In other words globalization can be balanced by regionalism. Second, since China is among the most active supporters of an idea of a multipolar world, it is quite logical for Beijing to be involved in institutionalization of economic relations in one of the most dynamic parts of the world economy. Growing activity of such countries as Japan and the ROK at the regional level is also a strong argument for China to focus its foreign economic policy on NEA.[10]

Development of bilateral economic cooperation between Northeast Asian countries became a very important feature of regional processes. It is necessary to note that rapid development of trade between NEA countries already reached high levels. The trade volume between Korea and China increased from a zero level at the beginning of the 1990s to US$80 billion in 2004. According to some estimates the volume of trade between these countries may reach up to US$120 billion by the end of the current decade. South Korean "chaebols" increased their expansion into the Chinese market. Under this process they simultaneously filled new export niches and relocated labour-intensive industries from the Republic of Korea to mainland China.

Economic cooperation between China and Japan has also increased significantly during the 1990s and at the beginning of the current decade. Their bilateral trade already reached US$100 billion and may be doubled by the end of this decade. Import of Japanese capital and technologies is vital for the future of China's development. In its turn Japan is interested in participation of Japanese firms in the industrial development of China.

Japan-South Korea trade is relatively small, about US$68 billion now. But quality, not quantity issues of bilateral economic exchanges are more important for modern Japan–Korea relations. Since 1998, Tokyo and Seoul have discussed prospects of establishing a free trade zone. Although two countries have not yet signed such an agreement, the above-mentioned bilateral Investment Agreement signed by Japan and South Korea in 2002 creates good legal and political environment for future development of economic relations between the two countries.

The share of Northeast countries in their mutual trade remains relatively modest. For example, trade with Japan and South Korea makes only up to 25 per cent of China's total foreign trade in 2004 (15 per cent in 1990), trade with China and South Korea makes respectively 16 per cent and 9 per cent of Japan's total foreign trade while trade with Japan and China makes up to 25 per cent of the ROK total foreign trade. Yet, in 2003–05, according to the World Bank, Japan's and the ROK exports to China increased by 47 per cent and 83 per cent respectively.[11] This growth of trade was stimulated by the PRC's accession to the WTO.

However rapid growth of economic exchanges in the triangle is accompanied by some negative consequences, such as "trade wars".[12] That is why the three countries try to work out adequate mechanisms of economic cooperation in order to prevent such "trade wars".

It is also necessary to emphasize that Beijing, Tokyo, and Seoul have some common foreign economic priorities that make it possible for them to coordinate their economic policies towards other economic partners and international economic organizations. Thus, China, Japan, and the ROK want to upgrade their role in the WTO by working out a coordinated position on international standards of goods and services.[13] The NEA nations maintain that Northeast Asian specific regional business and consumer practices, such as traditional business management, as well as labour relations, consumer demands and preferences typical for the NEA countries have to be taken into account in international rules and regulations adopted by economic organizations. Japan, China, and the ROK also pay close attention to cooperation on regional financial issues.

TRIANGLE NEGOTIATIONS: ISSUES AND PROSPECTS

At the end of the last decade, three countries realized the necessity of close consultations on economic issues between themselves. In order to overcome trade disputes, as well as obstacles for regional economic cooperation and to coordinate economic policy towards international economic organizations China, Japan, and the ROK decided to begin an intergovernment dialogue. Korean, Japanese, and Chinese leaders began to meet annually since 1999, and the number of issues discussed at their trilateral summits was growing year by year. Scale and speed of trade liberalization, support of investment flows between the three countries, development of human resources and monitoring of environment situation were among them.

In order to stimulate their cooperation the three countries initiated direct contacts at a working level (ministries and high ranking experts) since 2002. Special working groups focused their attention on such key issues as averting "trade wars", promoting investment flows, developing innovations projects, etc. Since 2003 heads of Central Banks of the three countries began to discuss financial issues on a regular basis. Several projects were initiated by the three governments in order to support direct contacts and cooperation between public organizations such as "young politicians".[14]

In the summer of 2003, President Roh Moo-hyun and PM Koizumi confirmed plans of their countries to sign a bilateral FTA in the near future. They planned to repeal tariffs on all kind of industrial (though not agricultural) products in mutual trade before 2012, to continue liberalization of investment regulations and to reach uniformity in national standards. Japan and the ROK were also planning to lift existing restrictions on the movement of labour between their countries. It is necessary to stress that Japan was inclined to sign a bilateral agreement with the ROK on these issues.[15] At the same time South Korea's attitude to such an agreement was more cautious. Some businessmen, politicians and experts were afraid of possible negative consequences of trade and investment liberalization for domestic industry. Annual deficit in bilateral trade of ROK with Japan is already about US$10 billion and according to some estimates it may increase as a result of expansion of Japanese business into South Korea. Nevertheless the South Korean government is inclined to continue negotiations. The Roh Moo-hyun administration believes that it would be easier to restructure national economy after the ROK signs an FTA with Japan as investment as well as technological bilateral cooperation may intensify.

In its turn, China is also interested in taking part in institutionalization of regional cooperation in NEA. At the annual summit of the three NEA countries in 2003, Beijing proposed to adopt joint declaration on economic and political cooperation between China, Japan and the ROK.[16] China also announced that in the future it was going to sign FTAs with Japan and South Korea. But an agenda of negotiations regarding such an agreement proposed by China was not transparent enough compared with the agenda of Japan–South Korea negotiations on FTA. Trying to explain China's position some experts believe that Beijing's regional policy towards such important economic partners as Japan and the ROK was still very cautious and reserved.[17]

According to the joint decision of the three Northeast Asian countries Chinese, Japanese, and Korean research centers analysed main regional economic trends and worked out proposals for the leaders of Japan, China, and the ROK in order to optimize future development of a triangle economic cooperation. In their published report, they came to a common conclusion that FTAs may positively influence Japanese, Chinese, and South Korean economies. Annual GDP growth rates may increase by 2.5 to 3.1 per cent in the ROK, by 1.1 to 2.9 per cent — in China, and by 0.1 to 0.5 per cent — in Japan. As research papers showed vast majority of business communities in China (85.3 per cent), Japan (78.7 per cent), and in South Korea (70.9 per cent) support the conclusion of FTAs between three countries.

Northeast Asian businessmen believe that trade liberalization and increasing investment flows may offer new opportunities for them to reduce production costs and to increase competitiveness of their business, both at home and on the global market.[18] At the same time, according to existing public opinion polls about one third of Japanese businessmen doubted that such an agreement may be signed with China within the next ten years.

Japan, China, and South Korea agreed in 2003 at their summit in Bali to implement jointly fourteen development programs in such areas as information and telecommunications, electronics, etc. They also decided to coordinate R&D activities and to improve cooperation in development of human resources (general and professional education, medicine and health care, cultural exchanges, and tourism). Besides Japan, China, and the ROK agreed to establish a special committee in order to monitor progress of triangle economic cooperation and to control realization of the joint programs.[19]

Each of the three NEA countries pursues, of course, their own priorities in regional cooperation in NEA. For example, Japan is interested in new markets for its goods, services and capital. Besides, structural changes in Japanese economy are closely connected with the transfer of some industries from Japan to South Korea and China. Triangle cooperation makes it possible for Japan to focus on the domestic development of high tech industries and services.

China's national economic priorities are also closely connected with cooperation with its Northeast Asian neighbours. Because of closer economic relations with Japan and South Korea, China has an opportunity to increase its export and to find new niches on external markets. It also helps Beijing to import capital and new technologies from the other two Northeast Asian partners. Another reason explaining China's increased regional activity is no less important than those already mentioned. For a long time China tried to avoid involvement in any international economic alliances because of its fears of foreign, especially American, negative influence on China's domestic affairs. This policy was changed at the turn of the twenty-first century. As a booming economic power Beijing initiated a more open foreign economic policy at the global and regional levels. China joined the WTO, made steps in order to establish close relations with Northeast Asian neighbours and with the ASEAN countries. It seems that China is now ready to play the role of one of the key architects of a regional economic community in East Asia. Realization of this strategy is expected to create better conditions for China's domestic market reforms as well as for its expansion in the global markets.

Main economic interests of the Republic of Korea in NEA are concentrated on improvement of relations with North Korea and establishing closer cooperation with China and Japan. This is necessary for a successful modernization of the Korean economy and optimization of national business structures.

Not only in the immediate future but also in the mid-term perspective, the activities of Korean businesses on external markets are likely to be focused on China and Japan. Seoul will try its best to use to its advantage its neighbourhood with these two great economic powers. It is quite logical that South Korea will try to play a role of a "regional hub" using for this purposes information and consulting services, transport, tourism, as well as some of its high-tech industries (for example IT and biotechnology). Simultaneously, Korea will try to expand the triangle of cooperation to the Korean Peninsula and mobilize Chinese and Japanese potentials for the reconstruction of the North Korean economy.

Because China and Japan are still wary about each other's foreign policies, both countries may welcome the ROK as a mediator and initiator of regional cooperation in NEA. As far as these three countries continue and expand coordination of their foreign economic policies not only towards NEA, but towards Southeast Asia, the European Union as well as towards other international economic organizations, the South Korean role in international relations may increase.

PROBLEMS OF TRIANGLE COOPERATION

Undoubtedly closer triangular cooperation positively influences economic trends in NEA. Nevertheless in spite of a rapid development lately of trade and investment flows between the three NEA countries there is still a lot of problems in economic relations between them undermining their regional cooperation. Also there are significant political differences between them that present serious obstacles for developing regional economic cooperation. Thus it is necessary to underscore that China's political system as well as China's foreign policy priorities differ significantly from political systems and foreign strategies of Japan and the ROK. These political differences cause periodical sharp political disputes between the three countries. It is worth remembering in this regard that six EU founding countries even at the initial stage of their economic integration were political allies, being members of NATO.

It also needs to be mentioned that economic institutions in China in many aspects still differ significantly from similar institutions in South Korea and Japan. Thus, banking and credit systems in China are still different from similar systems in two other countries. As long as triangle cooperation will develop, it will be necessary for China to reform some of these institutions. On the other hand both Japan and the ROK will have to adapt their domestic policies to new realities. Thus these two countries should improve their immigration policy in order to overcome labour shortages at home and make it possible for foreign labour to migrate freely in NEA.

Also, China's role in regional cooperation remains rather contradictory. Beijing is ready to open national economy, but is still very reserved at negotiations on legal and political issues. Transition of China from a closed to a more open society is an important factor of improving information, scholarly and humanitarian exchanges in NEA.

In spite of a substantial improvement in the state of economic relations within the triangle, the difficult history of political relations between the three countries still influences the agenda of their relationship.[20] Moreover, Japan's political relations with China and South Korea deteriorated lately quite significantly. Consequently trust and confidence among Northeast Asian countries remains at a low level. As a result it is very difficult sometimes to find out common basis for an agreement on some important economic issues, such as development of energy resources, because oil and gas fields are sometimes located in disputed border areas.

Nevertheless, it is very important that the three countries are not only eager to improve conditions for their regional economic cooperation and stimulate regional exchanges in many fields but also intend to coordinate their policies regarding other countries and such institutions as the WTO, EC, and ASEAN. Japan, China, and the ROK being among the leaders of world trade are ready to play a more significant role at multinational trade negotiations under Doha Development Agenda. If both Japan and South Korea support China in its efforts to adjust international standard and certification principles and procedures taking into account East Asian countries interests it would seriously influence the rules of the world trade.

In other words, relations between the three Northeast Asian countries remain rather complex. They are characterized by growing cooperation and partnership on some issues, and sharp economic competition and periodical political disputes on the other. Negotiations between these three Northeast Asian countries and ASEAN present an example of such ambiguous relations within the Northeast Asian triangle.

POLICY TOWARDS ASEAN: COMPETITION AND PARTNERSHIP

During 1999–2000 the ROK initiated consultations among the NEA countries in order to coordinate their negotiations with ASEAN member states and hoping to promote cooperation between Northeast and Southeast Asian countries. But South Korean initiative to work out some kind of a common agreement or at least a common position of Northeast Asian countries on the key issues to be discussed with ASEAN failed. It was too difficult for Japan, China, and the ROK to pursue a coordinated policy toward ASEAN at that time or to conclude a multilateral trade agreement with Southeast Asian countries.

Under these conditions Japan decided in 2002 to begin the process of institutionalization of its relations with South Asian countries on a bilateral basis by signing an FTA with Singapore. The choice was obvious: Singapore was a prominent partner of Japan in Southeast Asia; it was an industrially developed country and at the same time Singapore was neither among leading producers of agricultural commodities nor was it a substantial source of labour migration to Japan. In other words, there was nothing in Singapore's economic structure and policies to affect seriously Japan domestic agricultural and labour markets.

In its turn, China also started negotiations with the ASEAN countries with a view to form a free trade zone with Brunei, Indonesia, Malaysia, Philippines, Singapore, and Thailand by 2006, and with other ASEAN members — by 2010. There is no doubt that this decision deeply influenced regional activities of both Japan and the ROK.

Japan and ASEAN countries agreed to start negotiations on concluding their own FTA. As a result Japan's economic relations with six ASEAN countries (Brunei, Indonesia, Malaysia, Philippines, Singapore, and Thailand) may fall under FTA by 2012, and with other members — by 2017. It was also important for Japan to sign simultaneously bilateral FTAs with some of the ASEAN countries. For example, its bilateral FTA with the Philippines is now in the negotiation stage. An agreement with this country is especially important for Japan in order to control labour migration from the Philippines to Japan.

Following China and Japan, South Korea also began negotiations with ASEAN countries on concluding an FTA.

ASEAN countries prefer to keep Japan's and China's influence in Southeast Asia balanced as it is not in their interests to support a new rivalry in the region. It was logical that ASEAN countries proposed at their summit in November 2004 to hold annual East Asian meetings with participation from ASEAN, Japan, China, and the ROK. The main purpose of such meetings was to maintain regular discussions on key economic issues in East Asia. ASEAN countries tried to find out a new institutional form of multinational relations in East Asia and urged cooperation in order to establish an East Asian Community. Development of economic relations with the NEA countries under common rules would make regional cooperation for ASEAN countries more predictable and efficient. In any case, it may help to avoid confrontation and jealousy. In fact, this ASEAN proposal became an argument in favour of coordination of regional policies of Northeast Asian countries themselves and served as an additional important factor in favour of establishing a regional economic community in NEA.

*   *   *

Since the end of the 1990s, Northeast Asian countries are in the process of institutionalization of their regional economic relations. Negotiations between China, Japan, and the ROK at the high government level during

1998–2002 may be characterized as a period of their preliminary contacts. Step by step high-ranking officials, business organizations and academic research centers of these three countries also became involved into discussion of regional cooperation issues. Numerous meetings were held and special research programmes were conducted in order to work out joint proposals for intergovernment agreements on regional cooperation.

It seemed that the summit in Bali in 2003 became a turning point in the triangle relationship in NEA. Agreements reached between Japan, China, and the ROK at that time looked like a strong evidence of the beginning of a long-term economic cooperation among leading Asian economies. Realization of fourteen programs adopted there may be vitally important for the future of economic cooperation in NEA.

The next stage of trade, investment, science and technology exchanges in NEA may become an institutionalization of regional economic relationship. It will depend on the success of bilateral and multilateral negotiations between China, Japan, and the ROK.

The triangular cooperation will be in danger if Japan, China, and the ROK continue their political quarrels. Indeed there are many reasons to be afraid of such a scenario. Nevertheless it seems unlikely that the three countries would chose to undermine productive economic cooperation in NEA in order to achieve political goals because their political wins would be tactical and minimal while their economic losses would be significant and long-term. The scale and quality of regional cooperation is so important that nobody can ignore it, least of all the three Northeast Asian countries themselves.

As to concrete forms of their regional cooperation, it may not be necessary for the Northeast Asian countries to copy the European mechanism of regional integration. They may try instead to introduce a transitional legal and administrative mechanism of regional cooperation. It may consist of one or two general agreements, for example, on trade and investment regulation, including some elements of FTA, and several additional agreements on such issues as banking cooperation, joint R&D programs, environment, migration control, etc.

In other words it is in interests of each of the three countries — Japan, China, and the ROK — to get closely involved in a broad triangle economic cooperation even though the formal process of institutionalization of such cooperation may proceed slowly and in stages.

NOTES

1 Scolly R., "The Changing Outlook for Asia-Pacific Regionalism", *World Economy*, 2002, pp. 1142–43.
2 Ibid.
3 Bisley N., "The End of East Asian Regionalism", *Journal of East Asian Affairs*, XVII, no. 1 (2003): 158–59.
4 *Korea Herald*, 24 December 2002.
5 Kojima A., "Free Trade Agreements as Constructive Regionalism", *Journal of Japanese Trade and Industry*, January/February 2001.
6 Ibid.
7 *Nihon Keizai Shimbun*, 15 September 2003.
8 Kim Cae One, "Moving ahead with economic integration of North East Asia", *Korea Focus*, 11, no. 2 (2003): 97.
9 Ibid.
10 Chai Peng Hong, "Chinese perspective and the possibility of the China–Korea–Japan Free Trade Agreement", *Journal of East Asian Affairs*, XVI, no. 2 (2002): 220–21.
11 Hae Du Hwang and Xiang Shuo Yin, "The impact of China's accession into the WTO on the regional trade agreement in North East Asia", *Journal of East Asian Affairs*, XVII, no. 1 (2003): 175, 179.
12 The ROK tried to limit import of garlic from China and introduced in June 2000 custom barriers against Chinese exporters. In response the PRC immediately introduced the similar measures against South Korean exporters of mobile telephones and chemical goods. As a consequence of China's response, South Korea had to turn down tariff-wall. Similar disputes sometimes disturbed Japan–China economic relations.
13 Rhee Chong Yun, "Northeast Asian economic cooperation and Korea–Japan Free Trade Area", *Korea Focus*, 8, no. 4 (2000): 69.
14 *Korean Foundation Newsletter* 11, no. 4 (2002): 1–3.
15 *Nihon Keizai Shimbun*, 29 September 2003.
16 *Nihon Keizai Shimbun*, 28 September 2003.
17 Hae Du Hwang and Xiang Shuo Yin, "The impact of China's accession", p. 176.
18 www.koreaherald.co.kr08.10.2003, www.japantimes.co.jp08.10.2003.
19 *Nikkei Weekly*, 7 October 2003.
20 See: Rozman G., "Japan and Korea: should the US be worried about new spat in 2001?", *Pacific Review*, 15, no. 1 (2002); Kurklanzick J., "Is East Asia Integrating?", *Washington Quarterly*, Autumn 2001.

6

The United States and a New Stage of Economic Cooperation in East Asia

Vyacheslav B. Amirov

East Asia as a region has been traditionally of great significance for the United States. Now trade and other areas of economic interaction between the United States and East Asia represent one of the most important sections of the world economy. After 11 September 2001 (9/11), Washington has started to pay more attention to security issues in East Asia for obvious reasons. Because of that interdependence of economic and security issues, the importance of the region for the United States markedly increased.[1] Besides, China and Japan are two very important economic and political partners of the United States.

After the financial crisis of 1997–98, intra-regional economic ties in East Asia began to develop actively in various areas: trade grew significantly, particularly between China and the other countries of East Asia; new elements emerged in FDI exchanges; finally, a search in the region began for new institutional mechanisms to encourage bilateral and multilateral trade and other economic ties, making the region less dependent on external forces, and thus ensuring greater stability of the economic development of East Asia.

As the United States remains the biggest non-regional economic partner of East Asian countries, these new developments increasingly influence U.S.

relations with the region, and require from the changes in its long-term strategy in order to secure its presence in East Asia, and to engage regional countries more actively in the process of globalization.

U.S. ECONOMIC AND TRADE TIES WITH EAST ASIA

The volume of U.S. trade with East Asia is roughly equal to the U.S. trade with Canada and Mexico (combined) who are members of NAFTA and are most important economic partners of the United States. East Asia occupies a particularly important place in American imports where its share has been traditionally larger (with some fluctuations) than that of Canada and Mexico (combined). This fact shows a significant importance of the U.S. market for East Asian exports (see Statistical Supplement II, Table 2). The volume of trade between the United States and East Asia also greatly surpasses the volume of trade between the United States and the European Union (EU-15, see Statistical Supplement II, Table 1).

The size of economic ties (especially trade) achieved between the United States and East Asia and the mere scale of American economy make a fundamental impact on the economic situation in most countries of the region. It was proved beyond doubt at the end of the 1990s when East Asia was hit by financial and economic crises. Favourable economic situation in the United States allowed East Asian countries at that time to partially offset their economic decline and reduced intra-regional trade by export diversion to the American market.

It increased though, at least in the short-term, dependence of East Asia on the state of the American economy. Particularly important was the U.S. ability to import East Asian exports at the time when Japan experienced prolonged economic stagnation which significantly reduced its capacity to import commodities produced in East Asia (except Chinese goods).[2] China started to supplement Japan as an engine of regional economic growth only very recently. It remains to be seen whether it can replace or supplement Japan as a significant importer of East Asian commodities. Anyway, China more than doubled its imports from other countries of the region in 2000–03. As a result in 2003 China, for example, overtook the United States as the most important market for South Korean exports.[3]

Yet, any worsening of economic situation in the United States, as it happened in 2001–02, continues to affect significantly economic situation in many countries of East Asia while any improvement in the U.S. economy usually raises hopes in East Asia for economic growth, at least in the immediate future. It should be noted that in addition to direct trade with U.S. exports from some East Asian countries enter the U.S. market also via a third party, thus making the American market for them even more important.[4] The significance of the latter is clearly seen from dynamics of the U.S. share in exports of East Asian countries in 1996–2003. If, for Japan, that share has presumably reached its maximum level (which is now extremely high — about 30 per cent) and most likely will go down in the future, the role of the U.S. market for two other major regional economies — China and South Korea, increased substantially between 1996 and 2002: by 5.3 per cent points for South Korea and by 11.4 per cent points for China. For ten major East Asian economies, the United States continues to be the main export destination (along with Japan and, most recently, in some cases also along with China, Statistical Supplement II, Table 3).

On the other hand, East Asian share in U.S. exports markedly diminished in recent years (Statistical Supplement II, Table 2). The immediate future will show whether it is a result of the East Asian financial crisis and of its consequences (i.e., shrinking of domestic markets in East Asian countries) or it has been caused by growth of intra-regional trade that led to relative decline of U.S. exports to East Asia.

As U.S. exports to East Asia and U.S. imports from East Asia have been moving in opposite directions it has aggravated the problem of the U.S. trade deficit with East Asia. The region is responsible for about half of the U.S. overall trade deficit (Statistical Supplement II, Table 2), and a bulk (three quarters) of the U.S. trade deficit with East Asia goes to only two countries — China and Japan. That is why the U.S. government devotes particular attention to those two countries in its efforts to reduce trade barriers in East Asia for American goods and services and to improve business climate for American investments.

The other side of U.S. trade deficit with China and Japan is that both countries are the biggest holders of U.S. Treasury bonds. Japan was playing the role of a major holder of U.S. Treasury bonds for many years, but for China it is a relatively new phenomenon. This interaction makes a circle. Japan and China are interested in getting an access to the U.S. market. In return they actually cover substantial part of the U.S. federal budget deficit by buying U.S. Treasury bonds and using for that purpose their huge foreign currency reserves which are accumulated largely through surplus in trade with the United States.[5]

The scale of U.S.–East Asia investment ties are lagging behind the size of their trade, judging by a share of East Asia in U.S. overseas FDI (Statistical Supplement II, Table 4). During 1995–98 that share was particularly low, but later somewhat recovered when U.S. investors started to explore new opportunities of buying enterprises in Japan, South Korea, and some other countries of the region. In addition Tokyo, Singapore, and Hong Kong as main financial centers in East Asia maintain their attractiveness for American portfolio investors.

Anyway, the size of investment flows between the United States and East Asia cannot be compared so far with those between the United States and EU. The latter continue to be much bigger and therefore much more important for the United States (see Statistical Supplement II, Table 4).[6] It seems that, at least in the medium term, this situation will remain of relative importance for the United States, as investment ties with EU may even increase. But this does not deny the fact that FDI exchanges between Japan, China, and South Korea, on the one hand, and the United States on the other, have great potential. There are good chances for this potential to be realized, though that will require some time and additional efforts on both sides to improve the climate for FDI exchanges.

Among East Asian countries, Japan has closest investment ties with United States. The United States is the main destination and the most important source of FDI for Japan (Table 6.1). U.S. FDI in Japan's economy is relatively important. We say "relatively" because in general the role of FDI in the Japanese economy is quite limited, particularly if compared with FDI inflows in many other developed countries. In its turn, Japan is the most important investor in the U.S. economy among East Asian countries.

Table 6.1
The share of different countries in U.S. and Japanese FDI flows at the end of 2001
(in parentheses — share of relevant countries, per cent)

USA		Japan	
Total outflow	Total inflow	Total outflow	Total inflow
1 381 674*	1 321 063*	325 476*	54 572*
UK (18.0)	UK (16.6)	USA (47.6)	USA (36.8)
Canada **(10.1)**	Japan **(12.0)**	UK (11.0)	Netherlands (14.5)
Netherlands (9.5)	Netherlands (12.0)	Netherlands (6.5)	France (13.9)
Japan (4.6)	Germany (11.6)	Singapore (3.4)	Germany (7.7)
Switzerland (4.6)	France (11.1)	China (3.3)	UK (4.8)

* US$ million
Sources: U.S.–Japan Economic Partnership for Growth: U.S.–Japan Investment Initiative 2003 Report, May 2003 (www.state.gov/p/eap).

The United States is represented quite significantly as an FDI investor in some other countries of East Asia. For example, at the end of 2002 the share of U.S. in accumulated foreign investments in South Korean economy reached 21.8 per cent (the first place among all foreign investors), far exceeding investments from Japan (11.3 per cent) and from the Netherlands (9.9 per cent).[7] At the end of the 1990s, United States occupied the third place among foreign investors in the Chinese economy after Hong Kong and Taiwan.[8] According to Chinese official data the accumulated U.S. real investments in China stood at US$39 billion at the end of 2002. At the same time, the sum of approved U.S. FDI in China exceeded US$75 billion.[9] According to official Chinese figures, more than half of China's exports to the United States were carried out by Chinese companies, mainly with U.S. participation.[10]

U.S. ECONOMIC POLICY IN EAST ASIA: MAIN DIMENSIONS

General Regional Issues

An intensification of economic cooperation in East Asia at regional and sub-regional levels may result at some stage in the beginning of a real economic integration along the pattern similar to EU. It creates a new situation for the United States since, in the past, issues of regional economic cooperation were limited to the APEC agenda.

Since the very beginning of APEC, Washington made continuous efforts to secure its influence over the forum agenda. APEC was established as less "Asian" as it had been originally planned to be through invitation to APEC of a number of non-Asian countries in addition to the United States itself: Canada, Mexico, Chile and Peru — one after another. Since President Clinton proposed to hold the first APEC summit (Seattle, 1993), discussions at the forum started to be held at the highest official levels. It made APEC an influential global forum although decisions or statements made at its summits were normally taken as recommendations.[11] Nevertheless it helped the USA to bring new issues to the forum, although some of those issues were very remote by their nature from the original APEC agenda. The best example is the issue of international terrorism, which was brought to the attention of APEC by President Bush after 9/11.

At the time of its launch, the idea of APEC was that of a basically Western Pacific community. APEC was supposed to include as its members mostly countries of East Asia plus only two "whites" — Australia and New Zealand (their exports at the time were particularly dependent on the Japanese market). It was based on the economic might of Japan as the locomotive of economic growth in the Western Pacific. But the United States did its best to undermine an implementation of this idea, obviously wanting to control development of economic cooperation in Western Pacific or at least to obtain substantial influence over rapprochement between Pacific economies.

The U.S. interference in the process of APEC's formation encouraged some new ideas regarding the institutional framework of economic cooperation in East Asia. It was not by chance that the year after APEC was established (1989), Malaysia introduced its idea of an East Asian Economic Caucus (EAEC) with participation in it of East Asian countries only. Of course, it was not welcomed by the "white" members of APEC[12] and at that moment did not get much support from East Asian countries themselves.

But ten years later, at the turn of the century (and the millennium), as the result of new developments in the East Asian regional economy, particularly following the East Asian financial crisis of 1997–98 and the rise of China's economic power, the idea of establishing a community of East Asian countries emerged again — this time in the form of an ASEAN+3 dialogue. For ASEAN+3, contrary to APEC, the United States is an outsider and Washington has limited capacity to influence development of this new institution of regional economic cooperation. Therefore, it was bilateral relations with countries of East Asia where the USA still maintains strong economic and political advantages that have become more important for the United States.

After the East Asian 1997–98 crisis, disappointment regarding the lack of progress in trade liberalization within the APEC grew in the United States. From one APEC summit to another, statements in favour of collective support for "free and open trade and investment movement" were regularly repeated. But no real progress was achieved in working out a united position on the issues of the next round of the WTO negotiations. It seemed it was one of the reasons why the Bush administration started to pay more attention to bilateral free trade agreements (FTAs) with other countries.

One of the clear signs of a turn made in Washington's external economic policy in favour of FTAs was an article written by the U.S. Special Trade Representative Robert Zoellick. In this article, Zoellick underlined that by the end of 2000, the United States was still slow in concluding FTAs. There were already 130 FTAs in the world by that time, but the United States took part in only two of them, namely NAFTA and an FTA with Israel. Compared to the United States, EU had by that time agreements of such kind with twenty-seven countries and was involved in negotiations with fifteen more countries.[13] Zoellick's conclusion was obvious: America must catch up.

Before returning to civil service,[14] Zoellick had already been in favour of energetic commercial diplomacy with East Asia in order to remove existing barriers against the export of American goods and services, and direct investment.[15] So his stand on the matter as an official of the Bush administration came as no surprise. However, during the first term of the new Republican administration, the process of concluding FTAs between the United States and other countries did not get much speed, though President Bush was given by the U.S. Congress special rights for trade negotiations — the so called trade promotion authority ("fast-track").

Only in May 2003 did the United States signed the first FTA with an East Asian country — with Singapore. One month later, another FTA was signed with another member of APEC–Chile.[16] In both FTAs, the USA particularly insisted on inclusion into agreements mechanisms to solve problems caused by introduction of controls of capital movements. Interest in that matter was particularly expressed by the U.S. Department of Treasury. It was obviously caused by events related to the East Asian financial crisis when, for example, the Malaysian government undertook temporary measures to control or even to stop capital flows from the outside world. FTAs with Singapore and Chile set up a precedent for other agreements the United States wanted to reach with other countries.[17]

At the same time, a growing number of American experts started to criticize the U.S. FTA policy. They argued that the policy of bilateral agreements contradicted global development of free trade the United States had itself been advocating. According to FTA critics, such policy could instead reinforce bilateral trade protectionism and, besides, no country could be on par with the United States in bilateral trade and economic relations.[18]

Concluding an FTA with Singapore presented probably the easiest case for the USA since it was Singapore's leading trading partner, investment ties between two countries were well developed, economic and trade relations were not burdened by agriculture issues which usually are among most difficult problems to negotiate. In addition, both countries had close security relations. All these factors provided a favourable political environment for conclusion of an economic agreement.

After 9/11, the security factor started to play a particularly important role in U.S. foreign policy. During the Clinton administration, many politicians and experts in East Asia complained that the United States did not react properly to the East Asian financial crisis of 1997–98 (or simply stayed away). For the Bush administration, the importance of Southeast Asia for Washington has increased. The events of 9/11 led the United States to upgrade its attention to relations with Southeast Asia since countries of the sub-region, particularly Indonesia and Philippines, were suffering from terrorist activities and others were also not immune from this disease.

Along with strengthening security ties with SEA countries, the United States also started to explore opportunities for improving economic relations with them. After the APEC summit in Bangkok in October 2003 President Bush paid an official visit to Thailand that resulted in a bilateral economic agreement between the United States and its old ally.[19] There were also signs that Washington began to consider a multilateral economic agreement with ASEAN as a group.[20]

The most contradictory characteristic of the U.S. trade policy towards East Asia is a conflict between the U.S. desire to get concessions from regional countries in trade liberalization, particularly related to trade in services and agricultural products, on the one hand, and an active implementation of the U.S. national anti-dumping legislation and procedures against some most economically advanced East Asian countries, on the other. Restrictions imposed by the United States on steel imports from many countries, including Japan, South Korea, and China, was a typical example.[21]

The general atmosphere of economic relations between the United States and East Asia is under the influence of some specific, but very important issues like Washington's attitude towards emerging *regional monetary cooperation in East Asia*.

As East Asian countries came through the grave experience of the 1997–98 financial and currency crises, it encouraged them to undertake steps for creating an intergovernment institutional framework of regional economic cooperation and to make it more stable and less vulnerable to external shocks. It was meant to do so without participation of non-regional actors in it, including non-Asian partners in APEC (the United States being one of them). As a result, the beginning of ASEAN+3 process became the most important new development. It provided regional countries with a framework for discussing broad issues of regional economic cooperation and of future integration. It also led to such steps as the July 2001 Chiang Mai Initiative of bilateral currency swap agreements, and represented a move towards concrete protective (or preventive) cooperation among East Asian countries.[22]

Initially the United States reacted very negatively to initiatives aimed at developing monetary cooperation in the region, in particular to Japan's idea of establishing an AMF. It was rejected outright by the United States and IMF when it was proposed in 1997.[23] During the first term of Bush Jr. administration, the U.S. stance on AMF became more neutral, at least overtly. On the one hand, the Bush Jr. administration assumed a policy of a strictly negative attitude to financial assistance packages from IMF for crisis-ridden countries. The administration expressed its inclination to reject any help for countries, which found themselves in a crisis due to their governments' bad governance. The Bush administration stated that those countries did not deserve any assistance from the international financial community. At the same time, creation of some regional bodies such as, for example, a network of swap agreements in East Asia, provided the United States with an opportunity to stay away from countries-in-crisis and to transfer all responsibilities for assisting them to the regional level. According to that way of thinking, the idea of AMF might become acceptable for Washington. It remains to be seen whether this approach will be sustainable when and if AMF starts to become a reality.[24]

Relations with *Japan and China* present the most important challenge for the United States in East Asia.

A huge U.S. domestic market played a significant role in China's rapid and large scale "penetration" in international trade in the 1990s. It happened because Chinese exports entered the U.S. market both directly or via Hong Kong or as part of exports of Japanese finished goods to the United States. Since 1999 the United States became one of the leading destinations for China's as well as for Hong Kong's exports. The United States is now the second trading partner for China (after Japan).[25] In its turn, China became the third trading partner for the United States after Canada and Mexico (and the second after Canada as the main source of imports).[26] Since 2000 China also replaced Japan as the main cause of the U.S. overall foreign trade deficit,[27] which became a major issue in U.S.–China relations.

Under the Clinton administration, particularly during its second term, China was receiving increased attention from the U.S. government. It was a strategy to engage the "Asian giant" into global economy, to make China "a normal" participant of world economic integration and globalization, to open more widely China's domestic market for U.S. goods, services, and investments. It was believed in Washington that the easiest way to achieve those goals was to promote China's accession to the WTO.

The U.S. economic policy towards Japan during the Clinton years was different and more demanding. Washington often accused Japan of not doing enough to promote economic growth. During that period (except for the last year of Clinton administration), the United States continued to experience its largest trade deficit with Japan. Moreover during the 1990s, due to Japan's prolonged recession, exports from some East Asian countries were diverted from the Japan market to the United States, which also contributed to the growing U.S. trade deficit. The Clinton administration demanded Tokyo to remove specific Japanese domestic barriers for imported foreign goods and services. In fact, the United States started to push Japan to deregulate its economy and to restructure the whole system of government regulation of the domestic market.

When the new Republican team came to White House, it announced its intention to re-assess U.S. relations with Japan and China. Relations with Japan were again given the highest priority. According to a popular joke, many aspects of Bush Jr. policy were designed to be ABC (anything but Clinton). In the case of Japan however, this was most probably the United States real intention to underscore the importance of a close ally.

The Bush administration stressed that Japan was the leading U.S. partner in Asia (particularly bearing in mind the rise of China as a regional super power and anticipating increased prospects of an acute competition between the United States and China in the region in foreseeable future). It did not mean that the U.S. concerns about fundamental problems of Japan's economy disappeared. The Bush administration wanted to replace a "teaching" approach towards Japan (as it was under Clinton administration) with a comprehensive policy of bilateral cooperation in various fields. As a result, during the first term of Bush administration, U.S.–Japan relations strengthened considerably though it mainly applied to political and military ties.

The rising economic power of China and its consequences remained in the center of geopolitical concerns for Bush administration in the Asia-Pacific region. Initially, the new U.S. administration shifted the balance between strategic competition and economic cooperation in relations with China (this combination will determine, most likely, the U.S. policy towards China for years ahead) in favor of competition. However, in practice, while Washington pursued a "strong" policy towards China in political and military affairs, its approach of "economic engagement" of China was also maintained and developed. After some delay and mutual pessimism, an agreement on the terms of China's entry in the WTO was reached rather quickly and China became WTO member (December 2001) during the first year of Bush administration.

At the same time, the White House managed to convince the U.S. Congress to grant China a so-called permanent normal trade relations (PNTR) status, or a most-favoured nation status in December 2001. This decision abolished procedures which required that such a status had to be re-confirmed by the Congress each year after having debates on U.S.–China relations in various fields.[28] One of the main reasons for Washington to facilitate negotiations on China's entry in the WTO (which started in 1986) was to obtain a strong leverage on China to encourage Beijing to give up (of course, gradually) "unfair trade practices".[29]

Two approaches — one of containment, another — of engagement — continue to compete with each other in the process of working out the U.S. policy towards China. These approaches are clearly seen in official statements made by representatives of Bush administration. For example, Assistant Secretary of State for East Asia and Pacific Affairs, J. Kelly, making his statement in the Committee for Foreign Relations in the House of Representatives (25 June 2003), said that the administration considered China's integration into regional and world organizations as a positive development, though a growing economic power of China presented a challenge to the U.S. influence in the region.[30]

Some American experts on China expressed the opinion that Chinese policy towards the United States is more consistent than the U.S. policy towards China.[31] This should not surprise anyone who understands what a great difference exists between political systems and political traditions of both countries, including processes and mechanisms of working out external policies. But despite all these objective differences, fluctuations in the U.S. policy towards the Asian giant for the last five or seven years might be called rather excessive.

After China joined the WTO, the U.S. government, quite predictably, made observance of the WTO rules by China, in accordance with its obligations, to be a main direction of its economic policy towards Beijing. In fact, China was given about a year by the U.S. government for accommodation in the WTO, but since 2003, Washington started to increase pressure on Beijing on economic and trade issues. For example, in a speech before the Detroit Economic Club (15 September 2003), U.S. Commerce Secretary Don Evans said that the Bush administration felt that China was falling short in meeting its trade commitments. "We are waiting .... But we won't wait idly. We will work to ensure that China honors the commitments it makes", Evans said.[32]

Other direction of attack on China — yuan exchange rate. The U.S. argument is that the yuan is undervalued and because of that Chinese goods are artificially more competitive in the U.S. market. This is a popular complaint of U.S. manufacturing companies, supported by trade unions, claiming that the United States is loosing jobs to China. A group of U.S. congressmen even proposed a 27.5 per cent across-the-board increase of tariffs on imports from China, if there were no revaluation of yuan. But the issue is not that simple and because of that there is no agreement among American economists and economic observers whether these accusations are justifiable. For example, Nobel prize-winner (in economics, 1999) R. Mundell called the above tariff increase proposal a "very bad idea".[33] But the Bush administration could not ignore politically influential domestic voices, particularly before elections, and Treasury Secretary, John Snow and D. Evans were continuously and persistently, at least publicly, urging China to revalue the yuan.

It is an economic nonsense to determine that the yuan (or any other currency) is undervalued exactly by 27 per cent, 30 per cent, or by 40 per cent. But this is a tactic to fight economic competitors which was successfully used by the United States in the 1980s when they managed to force the Plaza Agreement (1985) on Japan in order to undermine its external economic power and which had quite serious consequences for Japan's economic development. In its reaction to the U.S. pressure, China cannot overlook the negative experience of Japan. Beijing easily repulsed accusations of undermining U.S. industry while saying that it was first of all U.S. companies themselves that were engaged in transferring jobs from the United States to China.[34] Not to say that, generally speaking, such transfer of jobs is an outcome of globalization, an objective process, which was promoted in the first place by the United States itself.[35]

The U.S. pressure on China on currency regulation and Japan's experience after it surrendered to similar pressure in 1985 encouraged some experts to think about a possible united stand of Japan and China on the Asian monetary system and Asian currency, though everybody understands that many obstacles exist along this way.[36] Though it is difficult to anticipate Japan–China joint coalition against the United States on the currency issue,[37] under certain circumstances pressure from Washington may encourage Asian major economic powers to promote an idea of regional monetary authorities within ASEAN+3 process to regulate currency fluctuations in order to strengthen East Asia's position in dealing with the United States. Swap agreements may be only the first but important step in that direction.[38]

Yet Japan's and China's approaches to U.S. participation in regional economic cooperation in East Asia differ markedly. China puts emphasis on a dialogue within ASEAN+3 advancing in the process such proposals for cooperation as an FTA between China and ASEAN. Japan, as an American ally, introduces a broader framework for regional economic cooperation, which may include "whites" — Australia and New Zealand (it resembles the original idea of a regional economic grouping put forward in late 1980s) and proposes openness for economic interaction with Europe and the United States.[39]

The United States faces attempts to form relatively closed regional economic blocks of one kind or another in East Asia in which the United

States will not be a full member in any case. It seems that representatives of every school of thought on China in the United States are convinced that China will continue to rise as a regional power at least, despite many domestic political and economic problems it has to overcome in the foreseeable future. The difference in opinions is whether to spend huge resources to contain the increasing Beijing appetites for a bigger international role or to continue to engage China in various international organizations, such as WTO, and to make it a "responsible" global player.[40]

There is no single opinion in the United States on who of the two Asian giants — Japan or China — is a more dangerous economic rival for the United States. In each case, the attitude depends on a concrete party: some may experience more pressure from the Japanese competitors, others — from Chinese.[41] That is why in practical policy in order to ensure long-term and powerful economic and political presence of the United States in East Asia, any Washington administration will have to take into account and to balance quite contradictory factors and interests existing in the United States. The role of the United States in the development of open multilateral economic cooperation in East Asia and broadly — in the Asia-Pacific region — will depend therefore on the balance between "protectionists" and "free traders" inside the United States itself.[42]

Statistical Supplement II, Table 1
U.S. External Trade Turnover by Countries and Regions

Countries/regions/years	2001		2002		2003		2004	
	U.S. billion	%	U.S. billion	%	U.S. billion	%	U.S. billion	%
U.S. total	1,873.0	100.0	1,856.8	100.0	1,983.1	100.0	2,286.2	100.0
East Asia (10)	**555.0**	**29.6**	**565.8**	**30.5**	**602.6**	**30.4**	**696.9**	**30.5**
Japan	184.2	9.8	172.9	9.3	170.1	8.6	184.0	8.0
Republic of Korea	57.4	3.1	58.2	3.1	61.1	3.1	72.5	3.2
Great China	196.7	10.5	219.4	11.8	252.3	12.7	312.8	13.7
PRC	121.5	6.5	147.2	7.9	180.8	9.1	231.4	10.1
Hong Kong	23.7	1.3	21.9	1.2	22.4	1.1	25.1	1.1
Taiwan	51.5	2.7	50.6	2.7	49.1	2.5	56.3	2.5
ASEAN (5)	116.7	6.2	115.3	6.3	119.1	6.0	127.6	5.6
Singapore	32.7	1.7	31.0	1.7	31.7	1.6	34.9	1.5
Malaysia	31.7	1.7	34.4	1.8	36.3	1.8	39.1	1.7
Philippines	19.0	1.0	18.3	1.0	18.1	0.9	16.2	0.7
Thailand	20.7	1.1	19.7	1.1	21.0	1.1	23.9	1.0
Indonesia	12.6	0.7	12.2	0.7	12.0	0.6	13.5	0.6
NAFTA	**613.6**	**32.7**	**603.7**	**32.6**	**629.2**	**31.7**	**710.3**	**31.1**
Canada	380.7	20.3	371.4	20.1	393.6	19.8	443.6	19.4
Mexico	232.9	12.4	232.3	12.5	235.5	11.9	266.6	11.7
EU (15)	**379.2**	**20.2**	**369.9**	**19.7**	**395.4**	**19.9**	**441.6**	**19.3**
Germany	89.3	4.8	89.1	4.8	96.9	4.9	108.6	4.8
Great Britain	82.2	4.4	74.1	4.0	76.6	3.9	82.4	3.6
Other	**325.2**	**17.5**	**317.4**	**17.2**	**355.8**	**18.0**	**437.4**	**19.1**

Source: Monthly Statistics of Foreign Trade, *OECD*, 2003–05.

Statistical Supplement II, Table 2
U.S. Exports and Imports by Regions and Countries (%)
(Round Figures)

Countries/ regions/years	1996 Exports	1996 Imports	1999 Exports	1999 Imports	2001 Exports	2001 Imports	2002 Exports	2002 Imports	2003 Exports	2003 Imports	2004 Exports	2004 Imports	2004 balance (− / +) U.S. billion
East Asia (10)	**29.1**	**37.2**	**23.7**	**35.7**	**23.7**	**33.4**	**24.3**	**34.3**	**24.7**	**33.6**	**24.5**	**33.7**	**−297.6**
Japan	10.8	14.4	8.3	12.8	7.9	11.1	7.4	10.4	7.2	9.4	6.7	8.8	−75.0
Republic of Korea	4.3	2.8	3.3	3.1	3.0	3.1	3.3	3.1	3.3	2.9	3.2	3.1	−19.8
Great China	7.1	11.8	6.5	12.4	7.0	12.7	7.7	14.4	8.2	15.3	8.9	16.4	−168.4
PRC	1.9	6.7	1.9	8.0	2.6	9.0	3.2	10.8	3.9	12.1	4.2	13.4	−162.0
Hong Kong	2.2	1.3	1.8	1.0	1.9	0.8	1.8	0.8	1.9	0.7	2.0	0.6	6.5
Taiwan	3.0	3.8	2.8	3.4	2.5	2.9	2.7	2.8	2.4	2.5	2.7	2.4	−12.9
ASEAN (5)	6.9	8.2	5.6	7.4	5.8	6.5	5.9	6.4	6.0	6.0	5.7	5.4	−34.4
Singapore	2.7	2.5	2.3	1.8	2.4	1.3	2.3	1.3	2.3	1.2	2.4	1.0	4.3
Malaysia	1.4	2.2	1.3	2.1	1.3	2.0	1.5	2.1	1.5	2.0	1.3	1.9	−17.3
Philippines	1.0	1.0	1.0	1.2	1.0	1.0	1.0	0.9	1.1	0.8	0.9	0.6	−2.1
Thailand	1.2	1.4	0.7	1.4	0.8	1.3	0.7	1.3	0.8	1.2	0.8	1.2	−11.2
Indonesia	0.6	1.1	0.3	0.9	0.3	0.9	0.4	0.8	0.3	0.8	0.3	0.7	−8.1
NAFTA	**30.4**	**28.6**	**36.3**	**30.1**	**36.3**	**30.5**	**37.3**	**29.7**	**36.9**	**28.8**	**36.6**	**28.0**	**−113.3**
Canada	21.3	19.5	23.7	19.4	22.4	19.0	23.2	18.1	23.4	17.8	23.0	17.4	−68.2
Mexico	9.1	9.1	12.6	10.7	13.9	11.5	14.1	11.6	13.5	11.0	13.6	10.6	−45.1
EU (15)	**20.5**	**18.0**	**21.9**	**19.1**	**21.8**	**19.3**	**20.7**	**19.0**	**20.8**	**19.4**	**20.6**	**18.6**	**−104.5**
Other	20.0	16.2	18.1	15.1	18.2	16.8	17.7	17.0	17.6	18.2	18.3	19.7	−137.7
Total (%)	100.0	100.0	100.0	100.0	100.0	100.0	100.0	100.0	100.0	100.0	100.0	100.0	—
Total, US billion	622.9	817.8	692.8	1,024.8	731.0	1,142.0	693.3	1,163.5	723.7	12,593.4	816.5	1,469.7	−653.1

Source: "The APEC Region Trade and Investment 2000", *DFAT*, (Australia), November 2000; "Monthly Statistics of International Trade", *OECD*, 2001–05.

Statistical Supplement II, Table 3
U.S. Share in Exports and Imports of East Asian Countries (%)

Countries	1996		1999		2000		2001		2002		2003[1]	
	Exports	Imports	Exports	Imports	Exports	Imports	Exports	Imports	Exports	Imports	Exports	Imports
Japan	27.5	22.9	31.1	21.8	30.0	19.1	30.4	18.3	28.8	17.4	24.9 (1)	15.6 (2)
Republic of Korea	16.7	22.1	20.5	20.7	21.9	18.2	20.8	15.9	22.0	15.9	17.7 (2)	13.9 (2)
PRC[2]	17.7	11.6	21.5	11.8	26.9	8.7	24.4	9.1	21.5	9.3	21.1 (1)	8.2 (3)
Hong Kong	21.3	7.9	23.8	7.0	23.3	6.8	20.9	6.8	21.4	5.7	18.7 (2)	5.5 (3)
Taiwan	23.2	19.5	25.4	17.8	23.4	17.9	22.5	17.0	20.5	16.1	18.0 (1)	13.2 (2)
Singapore	18.4	16.4	19.2	17.1	17.2	15.1	15.4	16.6	15.2	14.2	14.3 (2)	14.1 (2)
Malaysia	18.2	15.5	21.9	17.6	21.8	15.3	20.3	15.9	22.2	14.2	20.2 (1)	12.1 (3)
Philippines	33.9	19.7	29.8	20.7	30.2	20.6	28.2	18.4	28.5	20.0	21.1 (1)	18.8 (1)
Thailand	18.0	12.6	21.7	12.8	22.5	11.7	20.3	11.6	19.6	9.6	17.0 (1)	9.4 (2)
Indonesia	13.6	11.8	14.2	11.8	15.5	7.3	14.9	7.4	14.5	7.5	13.3 (2)	6.6 (3)

[1] In parentheses — the U.S. rate as exports and imports destination for relevant country.
[2] According to U.S. data the USA share in PRC's exports is much bigger than figures in this table, which are based on statistics collected by Asian Development Bank www.adb.org.
Source: "The APEC Region Trade and Investment 2000", *DFAT*, (Australia), November 2000; "Monthly Statistics of Foreign Trade", *OECD*, 2004; www.adb.org.

Statistical Supplement II, Table 4
U.S. FDI by Countries and Regions (U.S. million)

Countries/regions/years	1994	1995	1996	1997	1998	1999	2000	2001	2002
Total	73,252	92,074	84,426	95,769	131,004	209,392	142,627	103,767	119,742
East Asia (10)	11,746	8,156	9,986	10,595	10,752	25,531	21,683	14,468	24,095
	(16.0)[1]	(8.85)[1]	(11.8)[1]	(11.1)[1]	(8.2)[1]	(12.2)[1]	(15.2)[1]	(13.9)[1]	(20.1)[1]
Japan	1,867	2,336	(-) 280	(-) 339	6,428	10,602	4,295	2,322	4,482
Republic of Korea	390	1,051	752	681	631	2,557	2,338	1,345	1,446
Great China	3,922	1,311	2,913	5,711	2,730	7,404	7,690	6,539	3,822
PRC	1,232	261	933	1,250	1,497	1,947	1,817	1,225	914
Hong Kong China	1,979	631	1,690	3,759	1,880	4,447	4 922	4,407	2,035
Taiwan	711	419	290	702	(-) 647	1,010	951	907	873
ASEAN (5)	5,567	3,458	6,601	4,542	963	4,968	7 360	4,262	14,345
Singapore	1,836	947	2,760	3,697	261	3,863	3 688	3,820	11,407
Malaysia	553	1,037	1,298	733	(-) 470	(-) 250	1,787	(-) 4	936
Philippines	414	269	738	107	287	(-) 255	480	(-) 426	722
Thailand	703	686	849	(-)16	424	1,103	722	846	880
Indonesia	2,061	519	956	21	461	505	683	26	400
NAFTA	10,504	11,585	9,586	13,238	12,425	30,988	21,102	30,815	16,520
Canada	6,047	8,602	7,181	7,642	7,832	22,824	16,899	15,510	12,893
Mexico	4,457	2,983	2,405	5,596	4,593	8,164	4,203	15,305	3,627
Europe	34,380	52,275	40,148	48,312	86,129	109,484	77,976	44,720	66,761
EU (15)	29,762	48,835	36,182	46,910	75,771	97,815	70,625	39,625	55,553
Great Britain	9,615	13,830	16,421	22,961	29,094	47,265	28,317	15,720	18,871
Other	16,622	20,058	24,706	23,624	21,698	43,389	21,866	13,764	12,366

[1] Share of East Asia in U.S. FDI (%).
Source: U.S. Department of Commerce, Bureau of Economic Analysis, U.S. direct investment abroad (www.bea.doc.gov).

NOTES

1   This interdependence between American involvement in economic development of East Asia and American security interests in the region was stated numerous times by the U.S. officials even before 9/11. See, for example, statement of James A. Kelly, Assistant Secretary of State for East Asia and Pacific Affairs in the first Bush administration, *International Herald Tribune*, 3 May 2001.

2   Japanese imports from China in 2002 for the first time exceeded the country's imports from the United States. In 2003–04 China strengthened further its ascendance on Japanese market, "Monthly Statistics of Foreign Trade", *OECD*, 2003–04.

3   In 2004 a gap between export from South Korea to China and from South Korea to the United States increased further, "Monthly Statistics of Foreign Trade", *OECD*, 2003–04.

4   For example, some parts, components from China, South Korea or countries of Southeast Asian go to the U.S. market as components of Japan's finished goods.

5   "At the end of August 2003 Japan and China together held US$564.5 billion (share of China was US$122.5 billion) American Treasury bonds — almost 42 per cent out of whole amount of US$1.3472 trillion", *Asia Times,* on-line, 19 September 2003.

6   "In the second part of 1990s the USA–EU investment flows provided one quarter to one third of all world investment flows", *JETRO White Paper on Foreign Direct Investment 2001*, Internet Edition, Table 4, www.jetro.go.jp/it/e/ pub/whitepaper/invest2001/part1_1.html. There are also indirect signs of significance of bilateral investments. "At the end of 1990s sales volumes of American subsidiaries of EU companies were four times bigger than EU exports to the USA", *The Economist*, 24 March 2001, p. 97.

7   *Korea Now*, 8 March 2003, p. 23.

8   *People's Daily*, Internet Edition, 22 June 2001.

9   www.fmprc.gov.cn/eng/wjb/zzjg/bmdyzs/gjlb/3432/default.htm.

10   www.china.org.cn/english/international/75911.htm.

11   Some experts consider APEC rather as a process than an institution or a community because of its loose organizational form and consensus-oriented nature. See, for example, *Japan Times*, on-line, 31 October 2003; 8 November 2003.

12   At the same time while reaching agreement to turn U.S.–Canada bilateral free trade agreement into NAFTA with Mexico joining the two, Washington was planning to expand the new organization in future by taking into it Australia, New Zealand, Taiwan, Hong Kong, and Singapore. Governments and business circles of Australia and Japan — two countries, which were main driving forces behind establishing APEC, publicly criticized that intention, *The Australian*, 12 November 1992.

13   *International Herald Tribune*, 18 May 2001. By the June 2002 there were 143 FTA in the world (among them 117 FTA were concluded after 1990),

www.glocom.org/opinions/essays/20030430_pempel_future/index.html. According to other data, by the end of 2002 WTO was informed about approximately 250 of such agreements to be registered with the organization. If potential agreements were to be taken into account the number would increase up to 300, *Financial Times*, 13 July 2003.

14 He served at the Reagan and Bush senior administrations.

15 "Riding the Tigers: American Commercial Diplomacy in Asia", *Study Group Report, Council on Foreign Relations*, New York, 1998, p. 1.

16 *International Herald Tribune*, 8 July 2003.

17 *Financial Times*, 13 July 2003.

18 For example, see arguments of D. Wall from Institute of East Asia, Cambridge University, *Japan Times*, on-line, 29 August 2003.

19 www.state.gov/p/eap. In recognition of the close defense ties between the two countries, President Bush in 2003 designated Thailand as a Major Non-NATO Ally (MNNA), http://www.thaiembdc.org/fta/.

20 See, for example, *Japan Times*, on-line, 26 January 2003.

21 In November 2003, WTO made the final decision to declare temporary additional tariffs on steel imports introduced by President Bush for three years as contradictory to WTO rules. Japan, South Korea, and China joined EU, Norway, Switzerland, New Zealand, and Brazil in the statement welcoming the decision, *New York Times*, 11 November 2003.

22 By November 2004, 16 swap agreements have been concluded (two of them after expiring dates have been extended) with combined total size of US$36.5 billion, http://aric.adb.org.

23 Philip Y. Lipsky in his article in *Stanford Journal of East Asian Affairs*, 3, no. 1 (Spring 2003), described AMF proposal as widely unexpected. http://www.stanford.edu/group/sjeaa/journal3/japan3.pdf.

24 Initially China also rejected Japanese AMF proposal, www.glocom.org/opinions/essays/20030430_pempel_future/index.html. China rejected it for two likely reasons. First, it was strictly Japanese initiative, and second, may be, more important, China was not prepared at the moment to introduce its own initiatives for strengthening regional economic cooperation and wanted to earn time. As we know three or four years later Chinese regional initiatives on regional economic cooperation were put on the table.

25 Based on PRC official statistics, www.adb.org. It differs greatly from the U.S. trade statistics. In 2003, according to Chinese data, China's trade with the United States reached US$126.6 billion (exports plus imports) compared to US$134.5 billion for China–Japan trade turnover. According to OECD statistics (based on the U.S. national data), the size of the U.S.–China trade in 2003 was US$180.8 billion, "Monthly Bulletin of Statistics", *OECD*, 2004.

26 "Monthly Bulletin of Statistics", *OECD*, 2004.

27 "Monthly Bulletin of Statistics", *OECD*, 2001–04.

28 Wayne M. Morrison, "China and the World Trade Organization", *CRS Report*

for Congress, 6 August 2003; www.fmprc.gov.cn/eng/wjb/zzjg/bmdyzs/gjlb/3432/default.htm.

29 For example, the United States was against subsidies for Chinese industrial enterprises arisen from tax concessions, etc., www.cfr.org/publication.php?id=6255.

30 www.state.gov/p/eap.

31 www.cfr.org/publication.php?id=6255.

32 http://usinfo.state.gov. Evans said U.S. manufacturers have "complained about rampant piracy of intellectual property; forced transfer of technology from firms launching joint ventures in China; trade barriers; and capital markets that are largely insulated from free-market pressures". Evans also noted that American businesses are "still waiting" for the Chinese government to allow non-bank entities to establish financing arms so that Chinese consumers can purchase automobiles, a condition to which the Chinese government agreed when the country became a member of the World Trade Organization (WTO) in December 2001. Evans added that the promise of "free access to established distribution systems for American goods", being also part of China's WTO agreement, also remains unfulfilled.

33 Someone made calculations that yuan is undervalued exactly in that proportion — 27.5 per cent, *China Business Weekly*, 16 September 2003, www1.chinadaily.com.cn./en/doc/2003-09/16/content_265613.htm; *China Daily*, on-line, 23 September 2003.

34 *China Daily*, on-line, 23 September 2003.

35 As Elizabeth C. Economy, director of Asia studies at the Council on Foreign Relations, rightly said in one of her interviews on China: "… it doesn't do us much good to wring our hands and threaten tariffs. U.S. job losses and trade deficits are going to be part of the picture as long as China has 1.3 billion people, its labor is cheap, and its labor protection, environmental, and health and safety standards are much lower. Of course, the demand for Chinese products by the United States also has something to do with this trade deficit", www.cfr.org/publication.php?id=6255.

36 One of those experts is Mamoru Ishida, professor in the faculty of business, Hannan University. According to him: "There must be a reason for China's growing interest in a common Asian currency. It is time for both China and Japan to recognize that they would lose out in separate negotiations with the U.S.", *Japan Times*, on-line, 10 November 2003.

37 For political reasons, though many Japanese companies are involved in two-way trade in China and may suffer losses if there is a substantial yuan revaluation. Among them, for example, Toshiba, whose trade with China in 2003 was estimated as 500 billion yen, *Japan Times*, on-line, 13 September 2003.

38 Another small step in the same direction was the decision made in mid-June 2003, by central banks of East Asian countries and Australia and New Zealand to establish Asian Bond Fund to invest initially US$1 billion in Asian government

and quasi-government bonds with the idea to siphon excessive savings in Asia away from U.S. Treasury bonds and other dollar-denominated assets, and bring them directly to local businesses. One of articles on the event had a very impressive title: "QUIET UNION GATHERS MOMENTUM. Asian Bond Fund not just a pipe dream", *Japan Times*, on-line, 15 August 2003.

39   *The Economist*, 19 January 2002, pp. 52–53.

40   See, for example, Evan S. Medeiros and M. Taylor Fravel, "China's New Diplomacy", *Foreign Affairs*, November/December 2003. http://www. foreignaffairs.org/20031101faessay82604/evan-s-medeiros-m-taylor-fravel/china-s-new-diplomacy.html.

41   Some say that China represents the greatest threat and dollar/yen exchange rate does not matter, http://asia.news.yahoo.com/031103/kyodo/d7uisd5o0.html. Others accuse Japan in currency interventions to keep yen exchange rate lower and to undermine competitive advantages of U.S. manufacturers, *Japan Times*, on-line, 16 July 2003.

42   Public opinion in the United States is also divided on external trade issues such as loosing jobs to China, membership in the WTO or NAFTA, etc., *National Journal*, 11 October 2003, www.cfr.org.

7

Russia's National Interests and East Asian Regional Economic Cooperation

Gennady Chufrin

While exploring geopolitical and geo-economic realities in East Asia one has to highlight that national interests of Russia in this region are formed by the need: a) to maintain stability in relations with regional countries especially with those that are located either immediately on Russia's borders or in their close vicinity; b) to achieve and to maintain relations with all the regional countries at such a level when the latter would be directly interested in and would profit from Russia's development as a prosperous peaceful nation; c) to maintain economic security that would provide favourable external conditions for a balanced development of Siberia and the Russian Far East and for an efficient use of its natural resources.

Consequently, a large-scale engagement of Russia into the processes of economic cooperation and international division of labour in East Asia should be undoubtedly regarded as a matter of high national importance. Moreover, taking into account generally favourable forecasts of an economic development in East Asia, participation in economic cooperation with regional countries may present a unique opportunity for Russia to overcome the negative legacy of the Soviet times which resulted in over dependence of national export on energy products and raw materials, in a low competitiveness of domestic industrial products in international trade and in lagging behind industrial nations in modern technologies and know-how.

Also, the nation-wide role of transport infrastructure in Russian eastern regions was expected to increase since, as a result of the Soviet Union collapse, Russian western and southern regions were mostly cut off in the post-Soviet period from a direct access to international markets.

In June 2000, President Vladimir Putin signed the "Foreign Policy Concept of the Russian Federation" that contained a comprehensive assessment of the political, economic and security situation in which Russia found itself by the end of the twentieth century as well as an outline of national priorities in foreign policy at the beginning of the twenty-first century.[1] Among those priorities the "Concept" emphasized the need for Russia to actively develop economic, commercial and financial relations with countries in Asia which it described as one of the most dynamic region in the global economy. This goal was set in particular in order to speed up the economic growth of Siberia and the Russian Far East, an area having a critical importance not only for the future of the Russian economic development but in fact for the future of the Russian Federation in general.

Indeed, it is well known that this part of the Russian Federation possesses enormous wealth in natural resources, such as oil, natural gas, timber, ferrous and non-ferrous metals, and sea products. Thus almost 55 per cent of national proven recoverable reserves of oil are located in Western Siberia and 20 per cent more — in Eastern Siberia and the Russian Far East. Also Western Siberia possesses around 80 per cent of national natural gas reserves while about 10 per cent more are located in the Russian Far East and on the sea shelf of the Sakhalin Island. It is also well known that the massive export of these resources, energy products in particular, helped Russia during its most difficult years of the post-Soviet period to withstand a deep economic and social crisis and, in fact, to avoid a complete economic collapse. Moreover, even now, after Russia resumed its economic growth and achieved a respectable annual average growth rate of over 6 per cent in 2000–04, it is the export of oil, natural gas, ferrous and non-ferrous metals largely produced in Siberia and the Far East that continue to constitute the basis of Russia's foreign exchange earnings and its state budget revenue.

On the other hand the economy of Siberia and the Russian Far East outside of a few energy and raw materials producing and exporting industries stays in a depressed condition with low labour incomes and high unemployment rate. Among many negative consequences of such a situation is the worsening demographic crisis in the Russian Far East and Siberia characterized by the continuing reduction of the already very small Russian population of these areas[2] and by the growing illegal immigration from the neighbouring states. If these processes are not stopped and reversed, Russia may find itself in a fundamentally different security situation as early as within the next decade or two. Indeed Russia may lose sovereignty over these resource rich areas rather sooner than later not because of any sinister foreign scheming or an international conflict but because of the fact that even the basic needs and requirements of the local population have almost completely been disregarded for years by the federal authorities as well as because of a dramatic shortage of new investments in the regional economy.

Recognizing this threat, President Vladimir Putin spoke in July 2000 about an urgent need to offset it by launching a crash economic program for the development of the Russian Far East and Siberia.[3] It is clear however that in the foreseeable future Russia will be unable to carry out such a program relying only on its own technological and financial resources. No substantial progress in the economic development of Siberia and the Russian Far East can realistically be expected without promoting economic cooperation with neighbouring countries in the Asia-Pacific region in general and with those of them in East Asia in particular. It was quite logical therefore that the above-mentioned "Foreign Policy Concept" declared the goal of developing economic relations with Russia's neighbours in East Asia to be one of national strategic priorities.

Yet, the share of East Asian countries in the Russian trade for years remained at a very low level, of around 10 per cent of its total value, while the share of Russia in regional trade did not exceed 1 per cent of its value. Attempts that were occasionally made after the collapse of the Soviet Union to re-direct at least part of Russia's trade from western to East Asian markets appeared to be largely unsuccessful. Thus against initial expectations there was no serious change in re-direction of export and import commodity flows to railway terminals and seaports in the eastern regions of Russia. The reason given for that was that the dominant share of domestic industrial and public consumption was concentrated in the European and not in the Asian part of the country. Besides at the beginning of the 1990s this unfavourable situation was further aggravated following a radical decline in Russia's trade with some of its traditional partners in East Asia (such as Vietnam, Mongolia, and North Korea) caused not only by purely economic but also by political reasons. This mistake was realized rather soon but it was only since the second half of the

1990s that Russia began to restore its traditional economic ties in the region. Also contrary to expectations Russia's position on East Asian markets did not improve any visibly in the 1990s following establishment of trade and economic ties with new partners in the region, such as South Korea and Taiwan.

As a result, at the turn of the century, the state of Russia's economic relations with its East Asian neighbours were characterized by rather low levels of trade and direct investments. Moreover, by the end of the 1990s, the volume of Russia's regional trade actually stopped to grow with most of the neighbouring countries (China being probably the only exception) while with some of them, it even showed signs of decline. In order to reverse these negative tendencies and to give a new strong impulse to its regional trade Russia needed to introduce radical changes in its very character.

As processes of regional economic cooperation in East Asia were clearly gaining speed after the 1997–98 financial crisis, it was in Russia's national interests to develop economic and trade ties with its regional neighbours not only on the bilateral but also on the multilateral basis. To pursue these goals an active policy was needed that would help Russia to become an integral part of latest developments in the economy of East Asia.

One way to do that was to link purely commercial transactions to major industrial and transport projects in Siberia and the Russian Far East and to develop them jointly with participation of Russian neighbours. From the Russian perception such a linkage would both help to promote foreign investments in new industrial and infrastructure projects in Siberia and the Russian Far East and create the basis for more predictable and sustainable commercial deals with Russia's partners.

Among the most promising areas chosen for such a trade-cum-investment scheme became production and export of Russia's energy resources to its neighbours in East Asia. On the one hand, the energy consumption growth in East Asia countries was estimated by Russian experts to reach the annual rate of about 9 per cent during the next two decades.[4] On the other hand, the volume of domestic energy production in these countries was expected to lag behind their rapidly growing demands forcing them to increase their energy imports quite substantially. As a result, by the year 2020 their cumulative energy imports were estimated to exceed their present level by nearly 800 million tones in oil equivalent.[5] In this situation, Russia capitalizing on its geographical proximity, may realistically expect to become one of the principal suppliers of energy resources to East Asia countries.

Anticipating such developments in the regional energy market, Russia announced its intention to increase radically its energy production in the next few years in Eastern Siberia, at major oil deposits in the Yakutia and Krasnoyarsk region and at the Kovytkinsk condensed gas deposit (in the Irkutsk region) in particular. Also plans to build new oil and gas pipelines connecting these deposits with potential consumers in East Asia were initiated. Among these proposed projects was an oil pipeline from Taishet (Irkutsk region) to the port of Perevoznaya (near Vladivostok) via Skovorodino (Amur region) with the annual capacity of 80 million tones.

The decision to start construction of that pipeline was taken by the Russian government at the very end of 2004. Obviously that decision was taken above all in the interests of Russia's domestic economic development, in particular in the interests of a complex development of Siberia and the Russian Far East. At the same time however the construction of the Taishet-Perevoznaya oil pipeline may be of special importance for the future of Russia's business relations with its neighbours in East Asia.

Japan may become one of the principal beneficiaries of these energy production and export plans. It is now heavily dependent on energy supplies from the Middle East meeting almost 90 per cent of its oil requirements by imports from that region.[6] Clearly, transportation costs of importing oil and gas from Russia will be significantly lower and that factor enhances Japan's interest in cooperation with Russia on energy production and development. In fact, Japan is already strongly involved in developing oil and gas deposits on the Sakhalin island and on its sea shelf. By the beginning of 2004, its investments in Sakhalin energy projects already exceeded $2 billion. Also with the completion of the Taishet-Perevoznaya oil pipeline, Japan may import up to 50 million tons annually from Russia.

Similarly, China being one of the largest consumers of energy in the world, displays serious interest in developing cooperation with Russia. Thus China National Petroleum Corporation (CNPC) signed a contract in March 2004 for an annual import of up to 15 million tons of oil by railway.[7] Besides the CNPC was prepared also to become a shareholder in Russian oil companies and to make substantial investments in oil exploration and production in Eastern Siberia and the Russian Far East. On its part, Russia may build a special oil pipeline to the Chinese territory as an offshoot of the main Taishet-Perevoznaya pipeline in order to meet China's energy requirements.[8]

It is not only China and Japan but also other East Asian countries that may benefit from the construction of the Taishet-Perevoznaya pipeline or from the development of energy projects on Sakhalin island. They may include South Korea and Taiwan who already actively cooperate with Russia on energy issues as well as other regional states.

However, with all the obvious significance of oil and natural gas exports to the countries of East Asia, the future of Russia's trade and economic relations with them cannot and should not be reduced to these commodities. If Russia's cooperation with its regional neighbors is limited to exploration and export of its energy resources, only that would leave Russia in its presently passive role in the regional division of labour. It is clearly in Russia's national interests to change this situation. For that purpose, Russia is particularly interested in progressively changing the structure of its trade with regional neighbours by promoting sales of manufactured goods and sophisticated technologies. The Russian government, along with national private companies, should also undertake joint efforts to facilitate cooperation with East Asian neighbours in modern information and communication technologies.

In spite of earlier steps undertaken in this regard, Russia has so far largely failed to achieve a breakthrough into industrial markets of its regional neighbours. However, if Russia is prepared to undertake a more consistent and better coordinated policy aimed not merely at promotion of sales of its ready-made industrial products but also, by using such modern methods and opportunities as on-line procurement and outsourcing, at export of its software, at establishing production cooperation of bilateral as well as of a multilateral nature, at creating joint ventures with local companies, then it may reasonably expect to upgrade its role in the economies of East Asian countries.

For this Russia possesses substantial indigenous potential and retains a fairly competitive position in such areas as space, biotech and nuclear technologies or power generation and metal production to name only a few. Russia is prepared to develop multilateral cooperation with its East Asian neighbours on a number of transport projects — ranging from construction of gas and oil pipelines to creation of a regional railway network. Speaking about railway cooperation schemes, one should mention the already existing plans of linking railways of South and North Korea to the Tran-Siberian railway in Russia. After this project is implemented, it is expected to highly benefit the economies of its participants. It may also facilitate the establishment of a more stable and cooperative political climate in and around the Korean Peninsula and promote regional security.

In summary, one should underline that Russia has serious, in fact vital, economic interests in East Asia. To realize them it needs to develop bilateral as well as multilateral economic cooperation with its regional neighbours. Such cooperation may include joint development of Russia's abundant energy and raw materials resources. It may also focus on mutually beneficial cooperation in high-tech industries. As a basis for such regional cooperation, Russia is in the position to offer: a) its rich oil and gas deposits in Siberia and the Russian Far East; b) its resources of fish and sea products in its Far Eastern maritime economic zone; c) its sufficiently well-developed railway transport infrastructure that may facilitate transcontinental commodity flows from East Asia to Europe; d) its substantial industrial and scientific potential in the eastern part of the Russian Federation; e) its large pool of highly-skilled and relatively cheap labour force.

NOTES

1   "Kontseptsiya vneshney politiki Rossiyskoy Federatsii" [Foreign Policy Concept of the Russian Federation], *Diplomaticheskiy vestnik*, no. 8, 2000, pp. 3–11.
2   According to Victor Ishaev, Governor of the Khabarovsk region, during the 1990s the indigineous population of the Russian Far East contracted by 1,250 thousand people, or by 12 per cent, as the result of emigration to the European part of Russia, *Nezavisimaya gazeta*, (Moscow), 18 November 2002.
3   *Nezavisimaya gazeta*, 21 July 2000.
4   http://vestnik.tripod.com/news/latest/html, 8 April 2002.
5   http://www.transneft.ru/news.htm, 27 April 2002.
6   According to the International Energy Agency China, now already the fastest-growing consumer of oil in the world, is expected to increase its oil imports eightfold over its current import levels by 2030, http://www.nytimes.com/2002/09/03/business/worldbusiness/03CHIN.html.
7   *Kommersant*, Moscow, 10 January 2003.
8   http://www.rbc.ru/fnews.frame/20041231151252.html.

Index

.